Getting the Buggers to Write 2

KT-439-200

THE LEARNING CENTRE
HAMMERSMITH AND WEST
LONDON COLLEGE
GLIDDON ROAD
LONDON W14 9BL

WITHDRAWN

HAMMERSMITH WEST LONDON COLLEGE

338894

Also available from Continuum:

Related Titles:

Teaching Poetry – Fred Sedgwick

Teaching Literacy – Fred Sedgwick

Getting the Buggers into Languages – Amanda Barton

Other Titles by Sue Cowley:

Getting the Buggers to Behave 2

Getting the Buggers to Think

Guerilla Guide to Teaching

How to Survive Your First Year in Teaching

Sue Cowley's Teaching Clinic

Sue Cowley's A–Z of Teaching

Getting the Buggers to Write 2

Sue Cowley

continuum
LONDON • NEW YORK

Continuum

The Tower Building
11 York Road
London SE1 7NX

15 East 26th Street
New York
NY 10010

www.continuumbooks.com

© Sue Cowley 2004

All rights reserved. No part of this publication may be reproduced or
transmitted in any form or by any means, electronic or mechanical,
including photocopying, recording, or any information storage or
retrieval system, without prior permission in writing from the publishers.

British Library Cataloguing-in-Publication Data
A catalogue record for this book is available from the British Library.

ISBN: 0-8264-7314-8 (paperback)

HAMMERSMITH AND WEST
LONDON COLLEGE
LEARNING CENTRE

2 0 MAY 2005

338894   £13.99

372.623 COWley. 4

Typeset by BookEns Ltd, Royston, Herts.
Printed and bound in Great Britain by
Biddles Ltd, King's Lynn, Norfolk

Contents

338894

Part 3: Writing it Right

Part 4: Writing: Around the Subject

Figures

This book is dedicated to the children in my life:
Ania Giemza, Jessica, Rebecca and Elliott Castellino,
Jasmine and Sébastien Charman, Luke O'Gara,
Juliette and Matty Green.

And to Álvie Castellino, with all my love.

Acknowledgements

Thanks to all the brilliant English teachers who have taught me, worked with me and inspired me, especially Miss Ladd at Burlington Danes, Hilary, Valerie and the three Johns (Osborne, Browning, and Rust Andrews). Thanks to Anthony Haynes at Continuum for the great titles, and to my wonderful editor Alexandra Webster for all her hard work on my behalf. Thanks to Suzanne Ashley and Katie Sayers in Marketing, and to Christina Parkinson as well. And, of course, thanks as always to Tilak.

Introduction

Writing is fundamental: from primary to secondary school, in subjects as diverse as history, English, science and RE, we *all* have a stake in improving our students' literacy skills. Every subject taught in schools demands that, at some point, the student must pick up a pen and make marks on paper. Or, as we move further into the technological age, that they should boot up a computer and type their thoughts on-screen. How, then, can we 'kick-start' the writing process, whether this means getting the very youngest children working with the written word, or fighting the disaffection that some older students feel? How can we motivate and inspire our students to write, especially those for whom writing is a real struggle? And once we've got them writing, how can we ensure that what they produce is clear, accurate and well written?

This book aims to answer these questions. The material here will be of help to teachers working with young people of any age, in any area of the curriculum. The reactions to the first edition of this book tell me that this edition will also help anyone interested in developing writing skills, even beyond the world of education. In this second edition you will find lots of new material aimed directly at your own age range and subject; there are two extra chapters in this second edition. The first looks at ways of developing writing right across the curriculum subjects. The second deals with early writing, focusing particularly on material that will be of use for the primary school teacher.

In this book you will find a combination of tips, teaching strategies, examples and exercises, from which you can choose those best suited to your particular needs. Although it is packed with ideas for lessons, it is not a collection of lesson plans, nor is it a book on the theory of writing. Rather, the material here is designed to inspire you to find new and exciting ways to motivate your students to write. My own teaching experience has taught me that it is often the most unusual ideas and strategies that prove effective, especially when working with poorly motivated students.

My primary aim in this book is to offer you *practical* advice, written in an honest, accessible and straightforward way: advice that will be of immediate use to you in the classroom. The ideas included in this book are based on my own experiences as a teacher and a writer. I have tried to avoid jargon and complicated terminology, for these are the enemies of the writer and of the teacher. Our aim must always be to put across what we want to say as simply and clearly as possible, and for our students to do the same.

The National Literacy Strategy now reaches across both primary and secondary schools, and it is making teachers in all subject areas ever more aware of how crucial (and complex) the acquisition of literacy actually is. Within this book, you will find a huge range of ideas and suggestions that are linked closely to the requirements of the Literacy Strategy, especially as it concerns writing. The strategies and approaches that I give will help you teach writing in a way that will motivate and engage *all* your children, and allow you to give them access to the wonderful gift of literacy.

We write for a multitude of reasons and purposes. Some students write only because they have to, while others genuinely enjoy the chance to express themselves through words. The majority of our students are involved in written communication every day of their lives, although they might not realize it, or consider it to be 'writing'. Outside of class time (and sometimes even during lessons!), the sound of text messages being sent and received has become the new soundtrack of our school days. Emails and chatrooms, too, have become the technological equivalent of the paper messages that we used to pass around among our peers.

The reality for teachers in the classroom starts with motivating children to turn their thoughts into words, and to present these on paper. We need to show them that writing is important, and make it clear that there is no hidden secret to good writing, simply a range of techniques that we have to learn. Writing well is about learning the skills (and tricks) that help create good writing. Just as a violin player must learn musical technique before adding the expression that brings his or her playing to life, so we must teach our pupils the techniques that writing involves, thus giving them the freedom to express themselves both accurately and imaginatively.

Technique is not just about using correct grammar, spelling and punctuation, it is also about learning how to structure our writing, the skills of drafting and editing, the importance of dramatic tension in telling a gripping story, and so on. In this book I show how you can teach all these skills in an active, fun and exciting way to your students, and improve the writing of even the most poorly motivated children.

So, it is my hope that the second edition of this book will continue to help you in getting your students to write, and to write well. With the explosion of the internet, and technologies of all types, writing has become even *more* important, not less. By equipping our students to write well, we give them the best chance to succeed in life, to grasp all the opportunities they have to express themselves, and to contribute their ideas and thoughts to the world in whatever form of writing they choose.

Sue Cowley
www.suecowley.co.uk

Please note: To keep things simple, I have used a mixture of 'he' and 'she' throughout this book when describing students.

Part 1
Starting Points

1 The motivation to write

In every school, no matter how 'good' it is, there will be some students who are simply not motivated to write, or who find writing a huge challenge. You know the ones I mean: every word is a struggle, like getting blood from a stone, to use the familiar cliché. This chapter deals with different ways we can motivate and inspire our students to write, and ways that we can encourage them to keep on writing once they have started. Once this initial motivation is in place we can work on improving both the basics of their work, and extending their writing to a higher level.

Getting them writing

How, then, do we get our students to write? Here are some initial ideas and tips for motivating your children, which will work with all ages, and across the whole curriculum. Many of these ideas are explored in greater detail further on in this chapter.

- *Give them a reason to write*: When we ask our students to write, our motivation as teachers might be to cover the curriculum, or to help our class pass their exams. Don't forget, though, that children also need some kind of motivation for their writing. As far as possible, find ways to make the writing 'real', ways to inspire your students, to make them *want* to write.
- *Create an atmosphere for writing*: Aim to create an atmosphere in which writing feels easy and natural. This could be as simple as having a quiet, comfortable and positive working environment. It might also mean creating a 'mood' in your classroom that inspires your students to respond through the medium of writing.

- *Ensure the 'correct' behaviour for writing*: Unless your students behave, the atmosphere in the classroom will not be conducive to good writing, or indeed to any writing. To get your students writing properly, you will need to develop skills such as focus, concentration and self-discipline.

- *Make the writing seem like fun*: Make a game of some writing tasks, for instance using the format of a certain popular cookery programme. Use a stopwatch and prepare your class to start with the command: 'Ready, steady, write!'

- *Use 'warm-up' exercises*: When an athlete is preparing to run, or a dancer to dance, they warm up their bodies before they begin. In the same way, we can use 'warm-up' writing exercises to prepare our students to write.

- *Keep it topical*: Asking your students to write about something they find genuinely interesting will help motivate them. Utilize the latest craze as a basis for their writing, for instance the TV programme *I'm a celebrity, get me out of here* . . .. When choosing a text for your students, make sure it's up to date and engaging. The internet is also a wonderful and topical resource for inspiring writing.

- *Work to their strengths*: When you can, let your students write in the form or style that suits them. A good way of doing this is to use a group 'project' where different students work on different aspects of the task.

- *Challenge them*: In my experience, students are motivated by work that they see as really challenging – work that you might feel is above their current level of ability. Some pupils see English as a lightweight subject, in contrast to the more technical demands of science or maths. Defy this assumption: teach them about extended metaphors, iambic pentameter, pathetic fallacy!

- *Remove the stress*: Some of your weaker students might be fearful about writing, rather than lacking in motivation. Perhaps they associate a sense of failure with the act of writing, especially if they have a specific difficulty with technique. If this is the case, on occasions tell them to write without worrying about the technical aspects of their work, such as spelling and punctuation. This will free them up: they can always go back and correct mistakes later.

- *Remove the blocks*: Similarly, some students are 'blocked' in their writing, perhaps because of a fear of failure or of 'getting it wrong'. The 'stream of consciousness' technique (see p.11) offers a great way to free up their writing.
- *Offer a reward*: We all work best when there is a carrot ahead of us, rather than a stick behind us. Work out what will best motivate your students in their writing, whether this is stickers, merits or Mars bars. Have high expectations of what your children can achieve, and reward them when their work really deserves it.
- *Show that writing is relevant*: Talk to your children about the role of writing in their own lives: text messages, emails, the internet, magazines. Use these contemporary forms of writing as a resource to inspire your students.
- *Show that writing is important*: Talk to your classes about why writing is important, offering your own ideas and asking your students about their feelings. Talk with them about how we write for a whole range of reasons; for example, to communicate, for pleasure and self-expression, to remember things, to pass exams.
- *Show yourself as a writer*: Let your students see you writing as much as possible: on a blackboard or whiteboard, on an OHP, on their work. Articulate the writing process to show your class the intellectual steps that writers take as they work.
- *Offer yourself as an inspiration*: It is the teachers who were most passionate about their subjects and their teaching that I remember from my schooldays, the ones with that indefinable 'spark'. Sometimes we get bogged down in the minutiae of the daily grind, and forget that we have the ability to truly inspire our children. Show your students how much you love writing, and how excited you are about the work they produce.

Keeping them writing

Once motivated, students will often start to write with enthusiasm, but then run out of steam halfway through an extended piece of work. Here are some tips for keeping that motivation to write going once you have got them underway.

- *Set 'amount' targets*: Ask the class to write a specific amount, depending on their age and ability level, and on the type of task set. Your target might range from five words or one line of writing, to half a page or fifty words. For your weakest writers, put a mark on the page and ask them to write down to this point.
- *Set 'time' targets*: When you set a writing activity, always be specific about the length of time in which it must be done. Generally speaking, the shorter the time, the more focused the writing will be. Split up your lessons by setting short, timed writing tasks alongside a variety of non-writing activities.
- *Don't expect miracles*: Writing for a long period of time is counterproductive. Enthusiasm flags, exhaustion sets in, and the quality of the writing becomes poor. Even though I am a professional writer, I find it impossible to write for any more than half an hour before taking a break. Set your students a realistic length of time for their writing: fifteen minutes is about right to retain focus and energy.
- *Keep it fresh*: Give your students regular breaks when they are writing – after writing for about fifteen minutes give them a five-minute break to refresh themselves. This time could be used to discuss samples of the work so far, or for the students to chat with a partner about their writing.
- *Develop their concentration*: Good concentration is important when writing, especially if you have to write for any length of time (for instance in an exam). This self-discipline and focus is something that many students seem to lack. You can help your children develop their concentration by using the focus activities described in this chapter (pp.12–14).
- *Give them a test*: As exam time approaches, students often become much more focused in their work. We tend to offer our classes exam practice in the run-up to national tests and exams, but there is no need to restrict tests to these times alone. A test also offers the teacher a chance for a 'lesson off', although do stagger the setting of tests to allow for the additional marking.
- *Use unusual motivators*: In my experience, students are always motivated by unusual or imaginative resources or teaching

strategies. When approaching work on the Shakespeare play *Romeo and Juliet*, an excellent motivator I have used is to set up the story as a crime-scene investigation. The students then work as police officers to examine the evidence and interview witnesses.

Getting them writing properly

As well as having to deal with students who won't write at all, you will also find yourself dealing with those students who produce plenty of writing, but whose work is illegible, or has no punctuation, or doesn't make any sense. Here are some thoughts about getting your students to write in a meaningful and worthwhile way.

- *Show them why writing properly is important*: In order to communicate with an audience, our writing must be legible, clear and accurate. Demonstrate this to your class by using the following exercise. Ask your students to write down a short message, but with the wrong hand (i.e. the right-handed students write with their left hands, and vice versa). When they have finished, get them to swap with a partner for translation, and discuss the difficulties of reading and understanding.
- *Show them examples of 'incorrect' writing*: Looking at a piece of writing that is 'incorrect' demonstrates the difficulties this creates for the reader. One idea is to take a section of text and then tippex out all the punctuation. Studying the result will show your students how difficult it is to read without correct punctuation.
- *Share the work with the class*: Encourage your students to share, and even to mark, each other's work. If students know that their peers will be reading a piece of writing, they are likely to take care over it. In addition, they will start to get a sense of the type and quality of work that others are producing. (Be careful not to demotivate the very weakest students when using this technique.)
- *Share the work across the school*: Why not share writing across year groups as well? This is effective in both the primary and

the secondary school, for instance asking your students to write letters to their younger schoolmates.

- *Ask them to read their writing back to you*: Some weaker writers will finish a piece of work quickly, but will not bother to read it through (perhaps for fear of what they might see!). When students bring you pieces of writing that are illegible, or poorly punctuated, ask them to read their work back to you. The ensuing struggle should help them realize the vital importance of writing 'properly'.

A reason to write

Often, writing in school is guided by the teacher: 'I want you to write a review of the story we've been reading'; 'I'd like you to write up this science experiment for homework'. The piece of writing produced is then judged and graded by the teacher. Obviously this is necessary if we are to fulfil curriculum requirements and assess our students. However, it does mean that writing can come to seem like a chore and not a choice. Here are some ideas for giving your students 'a reason to write'.

- *Relate the writing to their own lives*: Many students now regularly use text-messaging on their mobile phones, so why not bring this form of communication into the classroom? Text messages also offer a very interesting insight into the way that language develops and adapts to suit its medium. Here is an exercise using text-messaging. Write the following text message on the board and ask your class to translate it.

RUOK? Y R U ☹? PCM. D8 2NITE? BCNU L8R.

(If you're not 'txt liter8' see Appendix 1 to find out what this says.) You might follow this up by asking your students to write a story using text-message abbreviations.

- *Make the writing fun*: Find ways to make writing 'fun' and educational at the same time. Try to think laterally – how could I approach this task in an unusual, humorous or imaginative way? For instance, students are often asked to 'write about yourself' as an introductory activity. A novel approach to this task is to ask your students to write their own obituary (including details of the horrific way in which they died). This gruesome idea captures their attention and offers an unusual way into a familiar topic.

- *Give them an inspiration to write*: You can get your children inspired by the use of imaginative resources or unusual ideas. Create 'fictions' for the class, for instance asking your children to bring in a favourite toy to interview, and then write the story that their doll or teddy tells them. Older children respond well to an inspiration that puts them in a position of authority, for instance that they are 'television executives' developing a documentary or drama.

- *Make the writing 'real'*: Writing at school can be rather contrived. Try and make it feel real – give it a genuine reason for taking place. You might get your students to write an email or letter to an author whose work they love, or to write to a local or national newspaper to complain about an issue of importance to them. If they are lucky enough to receive replies to their letters, this will give them added encouragement and motivation.

- *Use a group project*: Group projects allow each student more of a choice in the form and style of writing they are going to do, depending on their strengths or interests. If you offer a fairly wide choice of subjects for the project, each group can make their selection based on personal enjoyment and interest.

- *Set up a competition*: A writing competition is a wonderful motivator for student writing. In my first year of teaching I had fun setting up a whole-school poetry competition. You could choose one style of writing or allow a range of genres. This idea would work across the curriculum – for instance a competition for the best history or science project, or for the best biography of a well-known sportsman or woman in PE. Ask your school to fund small prizes such as book tokens to reward the winners. Publish the best entries in a pamphlet to celebrate the students' achievements and make them feel like 'real' writers.

An atmosphere for writing

Aim to create a 'mood' in your classroom in which writing takes place naturally. This might involve building an atmosphere that inspires your students or simply providing a quiet, positive place in which they can work. Here are some tips on how this can be done.

- *Set the boundaries for written work*: Right from the start, set boundaries for how written work takes place. You might feel that writing should always be done in silence, or that a low level of talk is acceptable. Perhaps your students write best when listening to music. Talk to your classes about their preferred atmosphere for writing, negotiating the boundaries with them. If older students genuinely work best when listening to music, you might allow them to use a walkman during written tasks.

- *Think about your classroom set-up*: Create a 'comfort zone' for writing, an environment in which external factors do not interfere with the writing process. Try to make sure that your students have room on their desks and are not constantly banging elbows with the person sitting next to them. Think about the levels of heat and light in your room, and how these might affect your children's writing.

- *Create a dramatic atmosphere*: An inspiring or dramatic atmosphere can really help to motivate your students. You might set the mood for writing a ghost story by blacking out the classroom and sharing some ghost stories with your class by torchlight, before the writing begins. You could develop this idea by playing a soundtrack of howling wind and creepy night creatures.

- *Use a variety of inspirations*: Again, think about unusual resources for inspiration: music, pictures, objects, etc. can all help create an atmosphere. Bringing in a prop of some sort helps inspire the students and engage their interest in the lesson. You might show the class a 'magical' box, and tell your students that it is locked shut, and cannot be opened (except by the right spell, of course!). The children could then write about what they imagine is inside the box, and subsequently write a spell to open it.

Warm-up exercises

Just as pianists play scales to warm up their fingers, or dancers do stretches to warm up their bodies, so writers need to 'warm up' before they begin work. The warm-ups described below cover both the physical and mental aspects of writing.

- *Finger exercises*: Some people suffer from cramp in their hands when writing for long periods of time. This may be the result of a poor writing technique, or of tension within the hands. Help your students overcome this by using physical warm-ups before you start written work. These finger exercises are also fun! Here is just one example, but there are plenty more that you can do (any pianists at your school will advise you). Ask your children to raise their hands in the air, palms away from their bodies. Now tell them to clench their fists tight, then spread their fingers as wide as possible, feeling the stretch in their palms. Repeat this several times.

- *Brainstorming*: Many teachers use a brainstorm to begin a topic as a matter of course, and this technique does provide an excellent intellectual warm-up activity. Gather together your students' ideas and note them on the board. This helps develop confidence in the less able, giving them some ideas to include in their writing. It also helps the more able to exercise their brains and decide exactly what they already know. Brainstorming is also a vital technique when planning longer pieces of writing such as essays.

- *Stream of consciousness*: Our minds are often full of back-ground chatter, thoughts and feelings that may be useful in our writing, but which often just get in the way. The stream of consciousness technique allows your students to 'tip out' the 'trash can' of thoughts that are in their heads – to clear their minds for work. It also helps them free up their writing. Set a time for this exercise – about two or three minutes is enough. When you say 'go' the students start writing, and they must keep going until you say 'stop'. They could write on a specific topic, or just write down any words or thoughts that come into their heads. If they get stuck, they should just keep writing the same word over and over again until they become 'unstuck'. Tell them not to worry about punctuation or spelling when they do this exercise.

- *Narrowing the focus*: This provides a good follow-up to the stream of consciousness exercise. It also helps your students to consider which words are more valuable or interesting than others. Take the initial stream of consciousness and ask the students to count the number of words on the page. They must then cut this number exactly in half, crossing out any words that seem irrelevant or unimportant. The writing does not need to make sense. When they have finished the first cut, ask them to cut the number in half again, so that they end up with exactly a quarter of the original word-count. Once they have done this, they might use the remaining words to create a poem, perhaps swapping or bartering words with other students.

- *Collaborative writing*: This is a fun way to warm up for a story writing activity. Give the students a single sheet of paper, and ask them to write the first sentence of a story on the top line. When they have done this, they pass the paper on to the next student, who writes the next line of the story, then folds the paper down so that only the sentence that they have written is visible. Some of the collaborative stories written in this way can be very amusing.

- *Picturing a story*: Again, this provides a good warm-up to a story writing activity. It also provides a useful focus for students who tend to 'dive into' their writing without thinking about it first. Ask your students to close their eyes and to picture the story in their heads, as though they are running a film. The teacher could tell them a story, or they could come up with ideas of their own, perhaps based on a particular topic.

Focus exercises

The following 'focus exercises' help develop the vital skills of self-discipline and concentration. They also provide good warm-ups for a writing session. They are based on drama exercises, but most should prove suitable for teachers in any curriculum subject. Some need an open space, while others can be used in a normal classroom setting. These focus exercises are extremely popular with children of all ages.

- *Hypnosis*: This exercise requires the students to focus on one thing for a length of time – the basic requirement for concentration. Demonstrate the exercise first by asking a student to come to the front of the class to be 'hypnotized' by you. Tell the student that when you click your fingers she will be 'under your power'. Hold your palm up so that it is level with her face, a short distance away. Once the student is 'under your power', she must follow you wherever you go, keeping her face at exactly the same distance from your hand. Move your hand around slowly, up and down, side to side, down to the floor, and so on. If you are brave, after demonstrating the exercise you can let the volunteer hypnotize you in return. Get the whole class to do the exercise, working in pairs.

- *Count down*: Again, this exercise helps set a 'focus' for your students. They should shut their eyes, and then count backwards from fifty to zero. When they reach zero, they can open their eyes and prepare to work.

- *Mental spelling*: Ask your students to close their eyes, and then spell a word or words backwards in their heads. For instance, you could start by asking them to spell their full names, then move onto key words related to the subject being studied.

- *Listening*: This is a very simple exercise to set a calm atmosphere before writing begins. Ask your children to close their eyes and simply listen to see what they can hear. At first, they could focus on sounds within the classroom, gradually moving out to sounds in the corridors, and around the school.

- *Puppets*: This drama exercise develops the skills of concentration, cooperation and coordination. Again, you could demonstrate it using a student volunteer. One person is the 'puppet-master', the other the puppet. The puppet-master moves his puppet around through the use of invisible strings, keeping his hand at a short distance from the part of the body he is moving. The strings can be attached to the hands, feet, elbows and knees. Alternatively, for an even higher level of focus, there could be strings on each of the fingers, on the head, and so on.

Putting the pleasure back into writing

The contrived nature of much of the writing in schools means that our students learn to see writing as part of the toil of the school day, rather than something that they might choose to do. We need to show them that it is possible to gain pleasure from writing, or to use it for self-expression. Here are some ideas about how you might do this.

- *Have a 'free writing' session*: On occasions give your students the chance to write purely for pleasure. Offer them a totally free choice of form and style – they can write about whatever they want, in any style or form they wish. During this session technique is unimportant – you are not going to be assessing what they write. Some students might choose to write notes to each other, others to write an article about their favourite pop group. Rather than marking the results, ask your class to share their work by reading it out loud. Talk to them about their reasons for choosing a particular form and subject and why it appeals to them. This will help you learn more about your students' interests – information that you can put to good use when planning your lessons.
- *Offer valuable rewards for good writing*: Depending on what motivates your students, whether it is merit marks or Mars bars, use these rewards to encourage good writing. The reward of seeing their work published can be a huge factor in giving your students pleasure from writing. There are many websites that publish student work (see Appendix 2 for some examples), or you could set up your own page on a school website to show off the best writing.
- *Display good written work*: Displaying good pieces of writing will help motivate your students. Remember to display the work of your less able as well as your more able students. If you feel it is necessary, get the student to redraft or type up a piece of work to correct spelling errors before displaying it.

- *Encourage keen writers*: There are probably students in your class who write for pleasure outside of school time, although you may not be aware of it. My own students have shown me examples of poetry, novels and autobiographies, asking for my thoughts on what they have done. Show your students that you are interested in any writing that they do, not just in the class assignments that you set.

The teacher as writer

Seeing their teacher as a writer is an excellent way of motivating students, and it will also help them learn about the processes involved in writing. Your students see you as a writer when you scribble notes on the classroom blackboard or whiteboard; when you teach them using an overhead projector or an electronic whiteboard; when you write evaluative comments on their work. Here are some ideas about the teacher as writer that you may find useful.

- *Articulate the process*: When teaching your class through your own writing, show that writing is an active process, one in which decisions are constantly being made. Comment on your own writing as it takes place. Talk about the thoughts that go through your head: how should I structure this, where should I put that idea, which words should I use?
- *Involve your students*: As you work on a piece of writing, ask for your students' ideas, involving them in the act of decision-making. Allow your students to contribute to the process, either orally or by coming up to the board and writing down their ideas.
- *Create a dialogue*: Use writing to set up a dialogue with your students. For instance, write a series of questions on a piece of completed writing, and ask the students to reply to your queries. This will help them learn more about the reviewing and editing process: how we decide what works well, and how we change things to work better. Another tip is to write a letter to each of your students about their writing and about targets for improvement. They could then answer your letter, setting some additional targets of their own.

2 The basics

The basics of language are the tools of the writer, just as a set of different coloured paints, and a selection of brushes are the tools of the painter. While students can express themselves reasonably well without getting the basics completely right, their writing will never be as good as it might be if they are not technically accurate (and of course they won't get such good grades in their exams!). This chapter offers you lots of thoughts, ideas and strategies to help you in getting the basics right with your class.

Traditionally, the job of teaching 'the basics' has taken place during 'English lessons' at primary level, or has fallen to English teachers in secondary schools. However, the Literacy Strategy asks that *all* teachers take a part in teaching good writing skills, and this is surely an approach to be welcomed. In this chapter you'll find lots of ideas that could be used with children of all ages, and within any areas of the curriculum.

Spelling

Just as when motivating your students to write, if you want them to spell correctly, they must understand why this is important. Talk to them about why we need accurate spelling for good writing.

- *Accurate communication*: Spelling properly means that our writing is correct and accurate and that it communicates exactly what we mean. Just as a chemist would mix up the proper ingredients for an experiment, so we must incorporate the correct ingredients into our writing.
- *Hiding the technique*: With really good writing nothing intervenes between the reader and what they are reading,

the technique is completely hidden. A skilled story writer immerses her audience totally in the fiction, until the reader feels as though the normal world has disappeared, and only the story world exists. If there are spelling mistakes in the writing, this could distract the reader.

- *Exam success*: The ability to spell properly allows us to succeed in our exams. Whatever the rights and wrongs of an emphasis on correct spelling, we (and our students) must accept that accurate spelling will indeed gain them better results. Be honest with your students – show them the marking criteria and explain exactly how their results will be affected by a poor standard of spelling.

Spelling difficulties

Problems with spelling can occur for a number of reasons, and it is well worth the teacher (of whatever age or subject) being aware of why errors occur. If we can identify the root cause of the difficulty we can put the relevant strategies for correcting spelling into place. Below are some of the reasons why errors may occur. You can find some suggested solutions to these difficulties in the following sections.

- *Special learning needs*: In some cases, for instance the student with dyslexia, the errors are a result of a specific difficulty. You can find some useful organizations involved in helping children with particular learning needs in Appendix 2.
- *A phonic approach to language*: Children who have learned to read with a strongly or solely phonic approach may try to spell words as they sound. This is fine for the phonic words in our language, but many words in English are not spelt in the same way that they are said.
- *A 'real books' approach to language*: Similarly, children who have learned to read without any phonic input will find it hard to sound out words, and to work out their spelling in this way. (Happily, the majority of schools now use a range of approaches when teaching reading.)
- *A lack of reading experience*: Constant exposure to words through reading will inevitably help with spelling. If we have seen a word spelt correctly hundreds or thousands of times,

we develop a visual memory of the correct spelling of that word. The child who has little interest in reading, or who finds it a struggle, will have 'met' less words than the keen reader, and will generally find spelling harder.

- *A lack of spelling strategies*: Some students may never have been taught any strategies for learning and remembering spellings. Teaching them these strategies will help them improve their spelling and also encourage them to look at the roots and structure of language.
- *Laziness*: Let's be honest: some children can't be bothered to check their work through for errors, or simply are not motivated enough to care about their writing to ensure that their spelling is correct.

Dealing with spelling difficulties

How, then, do we help our students when they have spelling difficulties? With the traditional method of rote-learning, and the weekly spelling test, they may well learn to spell a list of words. However, this type of memorizing is generally very short-lived, and without the strategies to retain the learning it is pretty meaningless. One of the most useful things we can do is to encourage our children to develop their own strategies for learning how to spell. Here are a range of tips and ideas to share with your class.

- *Study the words*: Digging deeply into language encourages your children to find ways of learning and remembering spellings. You might teach them to divide words up into syllables, or to search for the linguistic roots of unfamiliar words.
- *Use visual aids*: Labelling the 'things' in your classroom is a great way to familiarize your children with spellings. In the primary school this might mean labelling furniture and resources, in the secondary school it could involve labelling subject-specific items.
- *Use visual memory tricks*: Visual ways of remembering words can be very helpful. When working on the word 'bed' you could tell the children to make a 'bed' with their fingers. In this way, the children learn to put the 'b' and 'd' the correct way around.

- *Look at the shape of words*: Ask your children to explore the shape of the words that they are trying to spell. By examining the tall or short parts of words, or which come under or over the lines on a page, you give them a visual memory hook.
- *Find rhyming word families*: Connecting 'families' of rhyming words that are relatively easy to spell will help children remember vocabulary. At the simplest level, this might mean looking at 'at' words, such as cat, hat and mat. At a later stage in their schooling, you might use longer rhyming words, such as advance, perchance and enhance.
- *Use imaginative resources*: Using 'props' is a great way of sparking interest, for instance creating a display of science equipment, and giving volunteers the 'reward' of holding the equipment as the rest of the class learn the spellings.
- *Adopt unusual approaches*: Similarly, an unusual or lateral approach to spelling tasks can be very engaging. You might give your students a passage in which all the words are spelt phonetically, rather than accurately. The strange appearance of such a passage will make a very clear point about English spellings.
- *Use spell-checkers*: Using the spell-checker on a computer can be helpful when dealing with spelling difficulties, especially for children who are making only small errors in their writing. After all, why not use all the technology that we have at our disposal? However, be wary of the limitations of spell-checkers:
  - If the child's spelling is very poor, the computer may not be able to 'work out' the word that they are actually trying to spell.
  - Spell-checkers cannot help the uncertain speller with homophones.
  - There is a danger that the child might come to rely on the spell-checker, rather than using his own strategies to learn new words.
- *Use dictionaries*: As well as encouraging the use of dictionaries, do ensure you teach your children how to use them! Adults might assume that using a dictionary is straightforward, but it is in fact a skill that needs to be

taught. You can find some ideas for using dictionaries later on in this chapter (pp.36–8).

- *Create a sense of 'ownership'*: If we feel that we 'own' our learning, we tend to take it more seriously. To put this into practice, you might get your students to create their own lists of spellings to learn, ones that they personally find particularly difficult.

- *Supply the vocabulary*: The Literacy Strategy asks us to put a strong focus on learning new words and key terms across the curriculum. When first approaching a new topic area, make sure you supply your students with the words they will need. A great way to do this is to write a short list of 'key words' for each lesson on the board before you start. You can find cross-curricular vocabulary lists in Chapter 7.

- *Set regular tests*: Whatever the pros and cons of spelling tests, they do offer a useful way of analysing exactly where your children's weaknesses lie, and which words prove particularly difficult for individual students.

- *Encourage them to read*: The repeated exposure to vocabulary that takes place during reading will inevitably have an impact on spelling. Make the connection completely transparent to your children – let them know that the most active readers will generally be the most successful spellers and writers.

Top tips for learning spellings

The following tips will help students who find it difficult to learn spellings, and they are also very useful for any child attempting to learn a new word. By looking at words in detail, our students begin to understand the mechanics of the English language.

- *Relationships*: Relate the word being learnt to another word your students already know, thus giving the children a memory 'hook'. (For instance, 'obedient' and 'obey', 'prejudice' and 'prejudge'.) To develop this, you might ask your children to make a list of all words that are similar to a new spelling. They could do this by searching through a dictionary, or by brainstorming for ideas.

- *Find the words within a word*: Look inside a word, to find out what else is there. For instance, within the word 'courageous' we find the word 'courage', inside the word 'occasionally' we see the word 'occasion'.

- *Split words into syllables*: Splitting a word up into its separate sounds will help your students to remember a spelling. For instance, splitting 'February' up into 'Feb / ru / ary', or 'particularly' into 'par / tic / u / lar / ly.

- *Unusual sounds*: Many words in English are not spelt phonically (as we say them), or they have a hidden sound within them. In these instances, tell your students to emphasize the difficult part of the word in their heads, but as spelt, rather than said, correctly. In the two examples above, the 'ru' sound in February would be emphasized, and the 'lar' sound in particularly.

- *Memory links*: Links can be formed between some words and their spelling. To remember the word 'exaggerate' talk about the fact that it has two 'g's rather than one, to tie in with the whole idea of exaggerating. Similarly, the word 'too' means very and has more than one 'o'.

- *Learn letter combinations and sounds*: Certain letter combinations are common in English, and once their spelling is learned, they help children access and spell a wide range of related words. (For instance, the sound 'tion' at the end of competition, action, and so on. Similarly, the combination 'tious' at the end of superstitious, ambitious, etc.)

- *Use the roots of language*: Referring your students to the etymology of words helps them see the logic behind non-phonetic spellings. (For instance, the word 'beautiful' begins with the word 'beau', taken from the French. If we were to spell the word phonetically, it would be something like 'bewteafull'.) Look for patterns within different subject terminology, and explore where these words or letter combinations came from.

- *Study Greek and Latin roots*: Learning about Greek and Latin prefixes and suffixes can be very helpful. For instance, the prefix 'hypo' in 'hypocritical' and 'hypodermic', or the letter combination 'psy' in 'psychiatrist' and 'psychology'.

- *Picture the words*: The best readers are often very good at spelling too: they are able to see a word and know whether it is spelt correctly because they have seen it so many times in their reading. Encourage your students to visualize correctly spelt words in their heads, particularly those they find difficult. If a child always spells the same word wrongly, tell him to picture the wrong spelling in his head, with a huge red cross through it.

- *Learn the rules*: I have put this idea at the end of my 'top tips', because in my experience, unless a rule is especially memorable, children tend to forget it. In addition, some of the spelling rules we ask our students to learn are very complicated. A rule that has stayed with me from school (and probably with many of you, as well) is 'i before e, except after c'. We remember this rule because it rhymes, and this shows the importance of making spelling strategies memorable. However, even with this rule there is a complication. The rule in full is, in fact, 'words with an "e" sound have i before e, except after c'.

Some thoughts on homophones

Homophones or homonyms (words that sound the same, but are spelt differently) can prove a particular challenge for students (and sometimes for their teachers too). Finding links between the meaning of the words and their spelling makes them much easier to remember. Remember that the more unusual or wacky the idea is, the more memorable it will be. The following list gives just a few examples.

- *Here and hear*: This homophone is easy, because the word 'hear' has an 'ear' in it. Emphasize the point by asking your children to put their hand behind one ear and call out 'I h**ear** you!'
- *There and their*: Similarly, the word 'their' has an 'i' in it, and this can be related to the fact that it means 'belonging to'. Tell your students to remember that when they own something, they would say 'I own it'. This will help them to remember the 'i' in the word.
- *Words with 'ere'*: Words with 'ere' in them tend to be words related to place, for instance here, there, where. You might help your students remember this by using the phrase 'come over 'ere'.

Punctuation

The first priority when dealing with punctuation is to explain to our students exactly *why* it is so important to punctuate correctly. The areas that were identified for spelling apply equally to punctuation: we need to punctuate our writing properly so that we can communicate accurately and effectively, so that the reader can focus on *what* we are saying, rather than how we are saying it; and so that we can succeed in our studies and get the best possible results in our exams. Punctuation is also vital for finding a 'voice' when writing, and for expressing ourselves in the tone that we want our audience to hear.

one of the best ways to explore the need for correct punctuation is to show your students a piece of writing with all the punctuation removed ask them to try and read the writing out loud the difficulties that they experience in doing this will show the importance of punctuating properly in addition the weird experience of reading a paragraph that has no full stops commas speech marks or capital letters will help to emphasize how important punctuation is as we have seen a strange or unusual approach will often stick in the minds of your children im willing to bet that this paragraph has grabbed your attention

Problems with punctuation

Problems with punctuating correctly can occur for a variety of reasons, and again it is well worth the teacher understanding the possible source of the students' difficulties.

- *Lack of understanding*: Some children do not understand how and when different types of punctuation marks should be used. It may be that they have not been taught the 'rules' of punctuation early on, because they have forgotten them, or because they simply cannot be bothered.
- *Lack of experience*: A lack of understanding can also stem from inexperience in dealing with the use of punctuation. This may be because a child has had little previous experience of books and writing.
- *Over-enthusiasm*: When we are enthusiastic about our writing, it is easy to get carried away and write reams and reams but to forget to punctuate it. The ideas rush into your

head, one after the other, and you are desperate to get them down on paper before you forget them. Alternatively, an over enthusiastic writer might make excessive use of exclamation marks.

- *The 'and' disease*: Some children use the word 'and' as an alternative to dividing their work up into sentences. Again, this may be a result of over-enthusiasm, or because they do not know any other connectives and conjunctions to use in their writing.

- *Laziness*: Again, let's be honest: some of our students are not sufficiently motivated to check their work through for accuracy. Bear in mind that the ideal is always for students to punctuate *as they write*, rather than as an afterthought.

Dealing with punctuation problems

Here are some ideas and approaches for helping those students who experience problems with their punctuation. These strategies should be helpful at all ages where children are experiencing difficulties.

- *Explain the logic of punctuation*: Talk to your children about how punctuation helps us structure our writing. Show them how commas and full stops offer a chance to take a 'breath' when reading (either in their heads or out loud). Explore the way that a list of items is separated by the use of commas, and so on.

- *Revisit the rules*: Whatever age your students are, it is always worth revisiting the rules of punctuation. You might need to explore the use of colons and semi colons with GCSE students, or revisit the rules about commas with Year 6 children.

- *Read it back*: Asking a child to read their writing out loud, to you or another student, will force them to consider the need for punctuation. With a piece of writing that does not have any full stops this will prove very difficult.

- *Set targets*: For the child who experiences severe difficulties in punctuating, a simple target such as 'put a full stop at the end of every sentence' could be set.

- *Encourage punctuating while writing*: There is a temptation for students to go back and add in punctuation, rather than punctuating as they write. However, this approach re-inforces the weakness, and it is also a dangerous approach come exam time. Instead, try to encourage your children to punctuate each sentence as it is written.

- *Encourage the mental formation of sentences*: Ask your students to form each sentence in their heads (or out loud) before writing it down. This technique also helps with the skills of focus and concentration.

- *Develop the use of conjunctions and connectives*: You might brainstorm a series of connecting words or phrases to use in a particular piece of writing, or alternatively provide a list of 'sentence-starters' that give your children a frame to use in their work. Their first sentence could start with 'At first', their second with 'Next', their third with 'However', and so on.

- *Use 'cut and paste' activities*: This is an idea I have used to great effect. Pick a suitable passage and then go through it, tippexing out all the punctuation, noting each piece of punctuation you cut at the bottom of the page. Now ask your students to cut and paste in the missing punctuation, ensuring that they use up every full stop, speechmark, etc.

- *Make punctuation fun*: Punctuation can be a rather dry subject, so try to approach it in an interesting or lateral way. For instance, you might 'sell' your children a card with a certain number of full stops, commas and exclamation marks on it, and tell them to use it all up in a piece of writing. You could have a 'punctuation box' that the children can go to, to pull out 'their' punctuation.

- *Use active approaches*: Make the learning real and memorable by keeping it active. When teaching commas and full stops, you might give some of your children orange cards for commas and red cards for full stops. The class could then form sentences using these 'caution' and 'stop' cards to punctuate.

Some thoughts on apostrophes

Apostrophes do seem to cause particular problems for some of our students. Again, approach this problem by explaining the logic of the apostrophe: that it replaces a letter that is missing, or that it indicates ownership.

Here are two exercises specifically designed for teaching apostrophes.

- *The missing letter*: To demonstrate this rule, ask your students to write out the words in full, for instance 'it is' or 'they are'. Now tell them to cross out the 'missing letter' (preferably with a big red cross) and then replace it with an apostrophe to make 'it's' or 'they're'.
- *Belonging*: This way of putting apostrophes in the correct place is one that I still remember from my own schooldays. When trying to work out where to put an apostrophe, for example in the phrase 'the childrens books', turn the phrase around so that it says 'the books *belonging to* the children'. The apostrophe simply goes at the end of 'children', before the 's'.

Grammar

When teaching grammar as a discrete subject, it is vital to keep the topic as interesting and engaging as possible, especially when trying to motivate reluctant writers. Direct teaching of grammar has the potential to be rather dry, likely to demotivate those we most need to encourage. In addition to this, some of the rules of English grammar are incredibly complex and difficult to understand.

In this section you will find ideas for motivating your students to learn about grammar, and ways of teaching the topic in an exciting and original way. You will find some tips on an 'active' approach to grammar: getting students to work with their own writing, and with other texts, looking at the way in which words are used, the effects they create and how they might be changed. As part of this active approach, teachers can start to introduce grammatical terminology as a natural part of working with language.

Problems with grammar

When we are babies learning a language as our 'mother tongue', we don't sit down and study the rules of grammar with our parents. Instead, the rules are internalized through the process of actually speaking the language – using and hearing it on a daily basis. Knowledge about grammar, and grammatical terminology, might come about as a result of learning a foreign language, which could have different grammatical rules to English. For this reason, children who have been brought up in an environment where little Standard English is spoken may encounter difficulties with writing grammatically correct English. There can be a tendency for them to translate their speaking into the written word, for instance writing 'could of' instead of 'could have'. This problem highlights the importance of speaking and listening work, focusing on the use of Standard English.

Direct teaching of grammar

There is a tendency for some students to see English as a 'soft' area of the curriculum, one that does not require any real expertise, but simply the ability to put pen to paper. When teaching grammar as a discrete subject, explain to your students that English has its own technique, just as science or maths do. In order to meet the technical demands of the subject, they must learn about the complex nature of language – how to use it accurately so that they are freed up to develop the more imaginative side of their work.

As well as discussing technique with your children try to find some more original ways of studying grammar. It is tempting to use those worksheet exercises that ask the children to repeat a particular grammatical technique a number of times. However, although these are useful for reinforcing learning that has taken place, they do not always lead to genuine and lasting under-standing. Here are some more unusual ways of approaching the direct teaching of grammar.

- *Make it active*: We all enjoy learning that asks us to make an active contribution, rather than simply being expected to sit and write. Learning that has dynamic elements to it will stay with us longer, making more of an impact in our minds. Some children find understanding a topic via a verbal explanation very difficult, and this can be particularly so with the complex language of grammar. If I were to say 'today we will be studying comparative and superlative adjectives and adverbs, and the addition of the comparative and superlative suffixes "er" and "est"' you would probably switch off immediately. However, a teacher who asks for three volunteers to perform 'big', 'bigger' and 'biggest' will make an immediate and lasting impression.

- *Make it a group event*: Learning in which we take part as a member of a larger group also tends to stick with us. So, when teaching clause or sentence structure you might name each child in the class 'subject', 'verb' or 'object'. You could then put together sentences by asking the children to come to the front of the classroom and call out a word or words, working together to create the whole. So, the 'subject' child might say 'The girl', the 'verb' child could add 'bought', and the 'object' child might finish the sentence with 'a toy'.

- *Make it concrete*: Real objects can be powerful in the classroom. 'Props' can be very helpful in making grammar more real or concrete for your students. When exploring nouns, collective nouns, and singular/plural verbs, you might ask your children to each bring in a toy. You could then explore the difference between 'The toys are in the classroom' and 'A group of toys is in the classroom'.

An active approach to grammar

An 'active' approach is about letting your students have fun with the language that they and other writers use. By exploring the effects that different parts of the English language create, children can begin to experiment with their writing, and learn that working and reworking their own and others' writing is fun. In this way, the rules of grammar become internalized, by constant exploration and experimentation. In addition, use of grammatical terminology becomes a natural part of the process of working with language.

Here are some ideas for an active approach to grammar. These exercises cover only a few areas of the huge subject of English grammar, but they should give you some ideas for new approaches to the teaching of the subject as a whole. If you need information on different grammatical terms, you can find some useful websites in Appendix 2.

Working with other writers' texts

Below are some examples of ways in which your students might interact with the texts they read and explore the effects that other writers create by their use of words and grammatical constructions.

- *Playing with adjectives*: Ask your students to identify all the adjectives in a piece of text, perhaps with a highlighter. Discuss the effect that these adjectives have on the mood of the piece, for instance creating a scary atmosphere in a ghost story. Now explore the effect that changing these adjectives would have:
  - Can they find 'better' words?
  - What happens if all the adjectives are removed?
  - Is it possible to describe something *more* effectively without using adjectives?
  - What happens if they put in some 'boring' adjectives, such as 'nice', instead?
- *Avoiding adverbs*: You will find warnings in books on creative writing about adverbs being the sign of a 'lazy' writer. The use of an adverb to describe a verb lets the writer get away with not being specific about the action or the person doing it. Consequently this diminishes the picture that the reader might create in his or her mind. For instance, the phrase 'he walked slowly and fearfully up to the door' gives us an idea of how the character is moving, but is not particularly interesting or descriptive. Instead, the writer could say 'he crept up to the door, terrified that the floorboards might creak and give him away'. Again, you might ask your students to highlight adverbs in a piece of text, and come up with ways of rephrasing the text to replace them.
- *Exploring antonyms*: Go through a piece of text identifying all the adjectives, such as 'cold', 'big', 'happy', and so on. Now ask your students to find antonyms (words that have the opposite meaning) for these adjectives. Encourage them to find several antonyms for each one. For instance, the opposite to 'big' or 'huge' might be 'small', but it could also be 'tiny', 'minute', 'miniscule', and so on.
- *Exploring sentence length*: For this exercise, find a passage that

has a high level of tension. Tension is often developed by the use of short sentences, which might indicate a character's fear, or which could make the reader feel 'jumpy'.

- Explore the length of each sentence, looking for a series of short sentences that help heighten the tension.
- Which types of words are in these sentences?
- What is the shortest possible sentence available to a writer and what must it include (i.e. a single clause with subject, verb, object)?
- Now look at what would happen if these sentences were joined together with conjunctives, or if subordinate clauses were added.
- What would the effect be on the overall tension levels of the piece?

Working with their own writing
- *Prefix/suffix competition*: For this exercise, give your children a prefix or suffix, for example 'un' or 'ful'. Now set them a 'competition' in which they must find the maximum amount of words that can be made using this prefix/suffix in a set amount of time. These words could then be utilized in a piece of writing, or in a series of sentences.
- *Justify the choice of words*: When a student shows you a 'finished' piece of writing, ask her to explain her choice of vocabulary and grammar. Highlight any language that seems lazy, or that is grammatically incorrect. Ask the child to identify the type of word (i.e. adjective, adverb, noun, pronoun) and suggest that she finds a better alternative. Alternatively, explore with her why the words or phrases she has used are grammatically incorrect, and what must be done to change them. This technique allows you to focus on each individual's grammatical difficulties.
- *Brainstorm 'strong' verbs*: Having a bank of really strong verbs can be very useful, especially for creative writing. You could use a brainstorming session with your students, in which they find a long list of these words. (When I say a 'strong' verb, I mean one that indicates a forceful or energetic action.)

- Start this exercise by giving a sentence with a fairly weak verb, such as 'He threw the football at his friend'.
- Now look at all the alternative verbs that might be used, and the effects that these create.
- For instance, the verbs 'hurled', 'slammed' and 'thrust' would all offer a stronger, more active replacement.
- To make this exercise more active and fun, you could get two volunteers up to the front to demonstrate different ways of throwing a ball.

- *Changing tenses*: After your students have finished a piece of writing, ask them to change the tense throughout their work (or to swap their writing with another child and change the tense of his work). For instance, they might write a story in the present tense, then change it to the past tense. With older children, you could explore the effects of this process on viewpoint, tone and on the reader.

- *Ban 'sloppy' adjectives*: For a week (or permanently, if you want), why not ban the use of some of the more commonly used adjectives. (My vote would be to exclude 'nice', 'good' and 'very'.)

Some thoughts on paragraphing

In my experience, some students have a 'blind spot' when it comes to paragraphing. They produce reams of writing, but without a single paragraph in sight. Why does this problem occur, and what can we do to solve it?

The skill of paragraphing is essentially about learning to structure your writing: understanding the overall 'shape' of a piece of writing and the different ideas contained within it. Here are a few ideas about how you might develop the skill of paragraphing.

- *Write paragraph by paragraph*: When you are approaching a whole-class piece of writing, ask your students to write one paragraph at a time. You could set a sentence limit for each paragraph, and tell the class to stop when they have completed a set amount of sentences, perhaps four or five. They could then read out their paragraphs to the class, and discuss whether this would be an appropriate point for a new paragraph.

- *Identify the paragraph's point*: A single paragraph often deals with a single point, using a series of connected or related ideas. Ask your students to identify the points they are making within each paragraph of their writing, and where these points change from one set of ideas to the next.
- *Use the 'four-step' technique*: This technique for essay writing is explained in detail in Chapter 4 (pp.69–74). By using this approach, your students will create a series of paragraphs, each dealing with a single point or idea.

Handwriting

Handwriting is learned early, and any bad habits in the way that we form our letters, or hold a pen, will tend to stay with us long term. Here are a few ideas for working on handwriting with primary-aged children. (You may also find some of these ideas useful for correcting poor handwriting skills in older children.)

- *Use a pen-holder*: Pen- or pencil-holders help small children to learn a good writing position. These take the form of a small rubber 'sleeve' that is slipped onto the pen. Alternatively, some children may find that moulding plasticine around their pen or pencil will help them to hold it properly.
- *Consider the writing tools*: Using a ballpoint pen can cause difficulties with handwriting, especially for young children, as they may have to press very hard to form the letters. Look carefully at the writing tools your children are using, and consider whether they may find it easier to write with a felt-tip or a soft pencil, especially when they are first mastering the skill of handwriting.
- *Teach correct letter formation*: Most primary teachers will use demonstrations or worksheets that teach their children the correct direction and order in which to form their letters. I have found these worksheets helpful for older children, who have picked up bad habits when forming their letters.
- *Use active approaches*: This might mean working with a whole

class of primary children, drawing huge letters in the air to encourage correct letter formation. Alternatively, you could take a class into the playground and get them to write enormous letters in chalk on the playground floor, ensuring that they form the letters correctly.

- *Use ICT*: For those children who do find handwriting very difficult, why not give them a break at times by allowing them to write on the computer? This will enable them to concentrate on the content of their work, rather than on its presentation.
- *Teach calligraphy*: Make handwriting fun and a source of pride! By learning about the beauty of calligraphy, children can be encouraged to take pride in their writing and to see handwriting as an art form.
- *Explore other forms of writing*: If you have a parent who can write in Arabic, or a teacher in your school who can form Chinese characters, why not ask him or her to come into your class and help you explore different forms of writing and handwriting? Alternatively, you could study Egyptian hieroglyphics with the children.
- *Keep an eye on their technique*: Do keep an eye out for poor handwriting technique. If you are a secondary teacher, don't assume that all your students will have learned or maintained the proper technique. Children who are left-handed may find handwriting particularly difficult, as they will be covering the letters that they form as they write. Watch out for any difficulties they might be experiencing.
- *Explore graphology*: You will find some ideas for working on graphology below. These activities give a novel way of motivating your students to look at handwriting.

Graphology

The graphology exercises below look at what our handwriting 'says' about us. Using graphology will help you motivate your students to analyse their own writing, and that of others. It will also encourage them to consider the importance of presentation in writing and show them how our handwriting is as individual as we are. The subject itself is very complex, with many small indicators of personality, and the notes below offer only the briefest of guidelines for you to use in the classroom. (I make no claims to being an expert!)

There is some scepticism about the links between handwriting and personality. However, on a general level, graphology can offer some interesting insights.

- *Slope*: A forward slope suggests someone who pushes themselves towards people, while a backwards slope indicates a person who likes to keep people away. Upright writing tells you that the person is not really influenced by others, but has confidence in himself.
- *Flow*: Just as the way in which we move our bodies indicates our inner state of mind, so the way that handwriting flows can say a lot about a person. When the pen leaves the paper frequently, this shows caution and self-control. On the other hand, writing that flows smoothly shows a decisive, perhaps impulsive, nature. Words in which each letter is printed individually show someone with a visual awareness, and may indicate an artistic nature.
- *Pressure*: Heavy pressure on the page suggests a forceful personality, while light pressure shows more sensitivity. Tell your students to feel the back of the paper to check for the amount of pressure they are using. (They may be surprised to discover how hard they are pressing on the paper.)
- *Upper case*: This term indicates strokes which rise above the main body of the writing, such as the top of the letters t, l and h. A highly developed upper case shows somebody with a strongly idealistic, perhaps spiritual nature. People who do not create these developed upper-case letters tend to be more practical.
- *Lower case*: This term means the strokes that fall below the main body of the letters, such at the bottom part of y and g. These understrokes are connected with physical energy, the more pronounced the stroke, the more likely the writer is to be athletic.

Graphology: Activity 1

In my experience, students really enjoy this exercise, and particularly the challenge of working out whose writing they are analysing.

- Introduce your class to the art of graphology, using the notes given above. You could photocopy some notes and hand them out, or write them up on the board.
- Ask your children to write a short piece of text on a loose piece of paper. Either read the text to them, or ask them to write briefly on a subject of their choice. Warn them not to include anything that might help identify them. When they have finished writing, ask them to put a mark on the paper to help with identification later on (perhaps a number or a symbol).
- Collect in the pieces of paper, shuffle them, and ask a student to hand them back out. (Any children who receive their own text, or a piece of writing that they think they recognize, should hand it back so that you can swap it again.)
- Now give your students a set time in which to perform their analysis, using the graphology notes given previously. They could make notes on their analysis in their exercise books, but ask them not to write anything on the sample itself. (That way, you can use it with another class, if you want.) At the end of the time, they should try to guess whose sample they have been analysing.
- A good way to bring everyone's ideas together is to ask the students to stand up and give a brief analysis of the sample, and the person who they believe wrote it.

Graphology: Activity 2

I have found this to be an excellent motivational activity which grabs the attention of a class because it offers them the chance to 'analyse' their teachers. The preparation involved is worthwhile, as the exercise works very well with any year group, and can be repeated with all of your classes if you are a secondary teacher.

- Collect samples of handwriting from teachers and other people who work in your school by asking them to write out a short piece of text. Use the same text for each sample. Try to include some 'surprises', such as the head teacher, the caretaker or one of your catering staff. You might like to laminate these samples to protect them.
- Number the samples and make a note of whose writing corresponds to each number.
- In class, write a list on the board of the people whose handwriting the class are going to 'analyse'.
- Hand out the samples: your students could work in small groups on each piece of writing, swapping their sample with another group once they have finished.
- Compare the results, discussing your students' reasoning and rewarding those who have identified the 'correct' writer.

Working with words

The following ideas give you some interesting and engaging ways of working with words. I have used all these activities with my own classes, and they have proved very successful in motivating my students.

- *Hunt the word*: This is an excellent exercise for familiarizing students with using a dictionary. Introduce the activity as a 'game' or a 'contest', to help motivate your class. 'Hunt the word' can be done by individual students, students working in pairs, or by small groups, depending on the children's ability levels and on the number of dictionaries at your disposal. The teacher calls out a word, and the class must then race to find the word in the dictionary. As soon as they have found the word, they raise their hands and identify the page reference. You could extend this exercise by asking them to read out the definition, and identify the type of word (i.e. noun, adjective, etc.) You could also 'reward' the winners by asking them to choose the next word to be hunted. This game could be used with vocabulary from any area of the curriculum.

- *Invent the word*: You could begin this activity by looking at the poem 'Jabberwocky', which uses invented words, but ones that still make a kind of sense. For this exercise, ask your students to invent some words of their own. To help inspire them, you might suggest that they are aliens visiting the planet Earth, and that they have to invent words to describe the new things that they see, such as cars, television, houses, and so on. Their words should have some sort of connection with the things they describe.

- *Invent the language*: In a similar vein to the idea above, this exercise is good for a speaking and listening or drama session. The students work in pairs, using the following scenario:
  - Student A is a visitor to a foreign country, and does not speak a word of the language.
  - Student B is a local, who does not speak a word of English, only a foreign kind of 'gobbledegook'.
  - Student A must ask for directions in English, for instance to the bank.
  - Student B will then answer in the invented language.
  - After trying the scene, the students should swap roles.
  - Volunteers could then perform their scene to the class.
  This exercise can result in some hilarious improvisations, and also effectively demonstrates the different ways in which we try to communicate. After watching the performances you could start a discussion on how we use body language and gesture to try to overcome difficulties in communication.

- *Call my bluff*: This exercise is shamelessly ripped off from the television programme, and I have found it to be very popular. It is an excellent activity for looking at possible meanings of words via their roots, and would work with younger as well as older students:
  - Use a dictionary to find some unusual words.
  - Now divide your class into groups, and hand out one word and definition to each group.

- Each person in the group must then come up with an alternative definition for the word (of which only one will be correct).
- Taking it in turns, the groups then read out their definitions to the class, and the other groups must try and guess or work out the correct definition.

- *Word of the week*: For this exercise, choose one word per week for your class to look at in detail. To give a visual stimulus, you could get your children to make a huge poster of the word to go on the wall. Activities for the 'word of the week' might include:
  - The study of closely related words.
  - Exploration of the roots of the word.
  - Analysis of the category into which this word falls (i.e. verb, noun, etc.), and so on.

3 Writing techniques

This chapter offers an introduction to the basic writing techniques. I have included ideas about how you might introduce, teach and develop these writing techniques at both primary and secondary levels, and in a range of subject areas. Not every piece of writing will involve all of the techniques described below, but for extended or finished written work these steps are important in achieving the best possible result. Even the simplest piece of writing would benefit from a brief exploration of audience, viewpoint, and so on.

Writing processes

Below is a list of the main processes involved in approaching a piece of writing, and a series of questions for your students to ask themselves during each of the steps. You might like to give this list to your class to use when approaching a piece of writing. The techniques are organized in chronological order, in the way that they would be used when approaching a piece of writing. Some of the questions may be subject to the choice of the teacher, for instance the form of the writing and the audience at which it is aimed.

Preparing	
Find a starting point	*What can I use to inspire my writing?*
Select a form	*What's the best format to say this in?*
Know your audience	*Who is my writing aimed at?*
Think about your viewpoint	*Where do I stand in relation to my reader?*
Think about your style	*What kind of language should I use?*

Think about timing	*What tense and other time features do I use?*
Brainstorm your ideas	*What ideas do I already have?*
Research facts/ information	*What else do I need to know?*
Map your ideas/points	*How do these things connect?*
Select your material	*What do I need? What don't I need?*
Plan your writing	*How should I structure the piece?*

Writing
DRAFT

Review	*What's good or bad about it and why?*
Edit	*How can I improve my piece of writing?*

REDRAFT

Check for errors (proof-read)	*What technical mistakes have I made?*
Consider presentation	*What's the best way to present this?*

FINAL DRAFT

Review the finished product	*Is this as good as it could be?*
Evaluate the finished product	*How can I make it better next time?*

The three steps in capital letters do not have a question to answer: this is because these are the points at which writing is actually taking place. Your students may be surprised at how much else there is to do when creating a piece of writing. Some of the steps may be taken quickly, by making a decision. Others, such as redrafting, will take longer. It's a great idea to get your students into the habit of working through these processes when they write.

The following sections provide a more detailed explanation of each of these processes, and some imaginative, unusual ways of approaching them. I have included a variety of ideas for writing within a range of subjects and age ranges.

Selecting a form

In many instances, the selection of a form in which to write will be a decision made by the teacher. Finding an imaginative form for a piece of writing will help engage your children's interest. Imaginative, unusual forms can be used in all areas of the curriculum, as you will see from the three ideas given below.

- *Story writing*: (Infant Science) 'Teddy's Big Adventure'.
  - Teddy accidentally gets left behind by his owner, and decides to find his own way home.
  - In Teddy's way is a river, and he must work out how to cross it.
  - He tries various different materials to see whether they sink or float, so that he can make a raft.
  - The children follow up their research by writing the story of 'Teddy's Big Adventure'.
  - Using a real teddy, real materials and a water tank will make this activity much more engaging.
- *Interviews*: (Junior History) 'The Life of Martin Luther King'.
  - A study of the Civil Rights Movement in the United States, and specifically the life and assassination of Martin Luther King.
  - Students work as police officers, studying the historical data and conducting an investigation.
  - During the investigation, they interview witnesses to the crime, write up witness statements and police reports, and so on.
  - This work could lead to an exploration of the racist attitudes of some people at the time.
- *Film script*: (Secondary Geography) 'Environmental Disaster'.
  - Students write the script for a short film about an environmental disaster, for instance the *Exxon Valdez* oil spill.
  - They could incorporate extracts from television news reports of the time, or about current environmental issues.
  - They could also research the subject by writing to organizations such as Greenpeace.

- As with any play or film script, the chance to act out or video the work at the end of the process will increase your students' motivation and engagement.

Knowing your audience

It is vital to know the audience for a piece of writing, because this will help determine the language we use, the style in which we write, the type of presentation we use, and so on. Having a 'real' audience for their work is one way of truly engaging our students in the writing process. Here are some ideas about how you might find a 'real' audience.

- *Writing for others in your school*: As teachers, we have a real audience right on our doorstep, made up of all the other people at the school. For instance, in a mixed infant/junior school, you might:
  - Ask your students to write a book aimed at young children.
  - Invite a group of infant children into your junior class.
  - Get your children to research their specific needs and wants before preparing the books.
  - Read their finished books to or with the infants.
  - Obtain feedback from the children about how well the books worked.
  - Alternatively, your class could create books for a school library, or for the other teachers to read to their own classes.
- *Writing for the internet*: There are many websites that publish children's stories or poems, and this is an excellent way of motivating your students to produce high-quality work. (See Appendix 2 for some website addresses.)
- *Writing to a penpal*: Having a real person with whom to exchange letters or emails can be great fun. Your penpals might be:
  - Children from other countries contacted via the internet (again, see Appendix 2 for website addresses).
  - Students in other schools in this country.
  - Year 7 students in the local secondary school. (This is a

great way to help prepare Year 6 children for secondary school.)

- *Writing to an author*: Why not get your class to write to an author they admire? Some authors will respond to the letters or emails that they receive from their readers, and this can be a very inspiring experience for young writers/ readers.

Thinking about viewpoint

The word viewpoint basically means where the writer stands in relation to the reader. In a first-person narrative, the writer talks through the perspective of 'I', telling the reader about his own thoughts and feelings (or those of the character he is playing). Encourage your students to experiment with different viewpoints, exploring how a piece of writing works with either a first- or third-person narrative. Looking at different viewpoints is a great way to encourage the skill of empathy. Here are a few ideas for thinking about and working with a first-person viewpoint to help inspire you.

- *The toy's story*: Ask your children to bring in a favourite toy. Start off the lesson by showing them your own toy, telling the children its story using a 'toy-like' voice. The children can then tell the story about the day that their toys came to school, from the perspective of the toy, and using a first-person narrative. Extend this idea by asking your class to take the toys on a trip around the school, viewing the world through the toy's eyes, and considering its thoughts and feelings.
- *Diary writing*: Older students might write the diary of a famous person or historical character, again from a first-person perspective. This idea works well for an English lesson (for instance the diary of a character in a set text). It can also be used in other areas of the curriculum, such as history or religious studies.
- *The object's view*: A slightly more bizarre approach would be to use a 'character' that is actually an object. For example, your class might write from the viewpoint of the football

that was used during the FA Cup Final. How did the football feel about all those fans chanting? How did it feel about being kicked so hard, and ending up in the back of the net?

Studying style

There are many aspects that make up the style of a piece of writing. The writer's decision about style will depend a great deal on the form of the writing and the audience it is aimed at. Here is an activity for studying style that could be used at a variety of ages within the classroom:

- Ask your students to study several extracts of writing.
- Depending on their ages and the subject involved, this might include:
  - A children's storybook.
  - A literary novel.
  - A newspaper report.
  - A history textbook.
  - A recipe.
- Now ask them to examine the style that the writer uses in these extracts, using the checklist given below.
- When they have completed their study, discuss the effect of these different aspects of style.
- After working on the extracts, follow up the activity by asking the children to rewrite the piece, but in a completely different style.
- Ask them to choose a totally different audience for their work.
- For instance, a 'dry' piece of writing from a history textbook could be written in the style of a football match report.

Studying Style: Checklist

Audience:
- What type of audience is this writing aimed at?
- How old is the projected audience? How can we tell this?
- Is the piece successful in appealing to this audience?

Language:
- What type of vocabulary does the writer use?
- Are there long or short words, or a mixture of both?
- Will the audience understand the words that are used?
- Is the writer trying to sound 'clever'?

Grammar:
- Is Standard English used, and is the writing grammatically correct?
- Is a more formal, or talkative style apparent?
- How does the grammar relate to the form and audience of the piece?

Formal or informal
- Does the writer use formal or informal language?
- Which words tell you this?
- Why has a formal or informal style been chosen?

Interest level:
- Is the writing interesting or gripping for the reader?
- What is it about the style of the piece that creates this interest level?

Genre:
- Is the piece of writing in a particular genre, involving a certain type of mood?
- What type of mood is created?
- Which words or images tell you about the genre?

Tone:
- Does the writer 'sound' as though she is in a particular mood?
- Is the style of the piece 'happy' or 'sad', 'calm' or 'angry'?
- Is the writer trying to evoke a specific emotion in her audience?

Thinking about timing

An important step in the writing process is to work out a 'time setting' for the writing. One of the key features of timing is clearly the ability to write in (and stick to) the correct tense. This is something that many of our students do find very hard. As well as considering which tense to use, you can also encourage your children to play with other aspects of timing, particularly when writing a creative piece.

It is helpful for your students to understand the reasons behind the logic of tenses. With the use of tense writers need to think about where they stand in relation to the piece of writing. Are they describing something that happened in the past, that is happening in the present, or that will happen in the future? Here are some thoughts about the logic behind tenses that you could share with your class.

- *The story*: The majority of stories are written in the past tense. To help your children understand why this is, talk about the imaginative process of inventing a story. The best stories are created first in our heads, rather than being made up as we write. Encourage your children (however young they are) to run a 'film' of the story in their imagination, 'watching' the characters and the events that take place. Then, the process of writing the story becomes simply a case of describing the events that have just taken place, in (of course) the past tense.

- *The essay*: When we are writing an essay, unless we are describing historical events that have taken place in the past, we are giving an interpretation of a text or situation, or making a series of statements that we believe to be true. These interpretations or statements are made at the moment we write the essay. Consequently, the present tense is the logical tense to use.

- *Instructions*: If we are writing a list of instructions to build a piece of furniture, we are describing the series of actions that somebody would need to take in their 'present'. Consequently, we would use the present tense, for instance 'First, nail the wooden board into the base ...'. If the instructions were details of a forthcoming school trip, the future tense

might be used, for instance 'next week we will be going to
. . .'.

In addition to considerations about the correct tense,
encourage your students to think carefully about the timing and
pace of their writing. This is particularly helpful for the writing of
fiction. The ideas and examples below give you an insight into
how pace is created.

- *A balance of description and action*: The pace of a piece of
  writing depends a great deal on the balance of these two
  features. If a story is heavily descriptive, this will slow the
  pace right down for the reader. A story that is pure action,
  without even an adjective to slow things down, will be
  fast-paced and gripping. You could ask your students to
  write a close, descriptive study, and then a fast, pure action
  story.
- *Slow-motion moments*: Many films make use of slow motion at
  a pivotal point in the story. Encourage your students to
  consider which moments in their writing might deserve the
  'slo-mo' treatment and why.
- *Sentence length*: The length of the sentences in a piece of
  writing will have a surprisingly strong impact on its pace.
  Long sentences tend to slow down the pace of the writing,
  allowing readers to 'sit back' as they picture the story. Short
  sentences add pace and movement to writing, and help
  develop an edgy, tense feeling.
- *Punctuation*: Punctuation has a strong influence on the pace
  of writing. A sentence divided up using lots of commas will
  slow the reader down, as each comma signals a pause for
  breath.

The two examples below demonstrate how description can
slow the pace down while a more action-packed style will give a
piece that reads at a faster pace.

Example 1: Descriptive (slow pace)
Jane stood in front of the doorway, collecting her thoughts, delaying her decision until the last possible moment. As she waited for her courage to arrive, like a slow train moving into the last station on the line, she studied the door in front of her. It was crafted from ancient-looking wood, the handle a simple metal ring. Jane glanced down as she stretched her arm out towards the handle. Her hand was shaking, and the deep red nail polish on her nails reminded her of blood. She retracted her hand and took two deep breaths, brushing her fringe from her face with her pale fingers. She stood a while, contemplating everything that might happen once she went inside. Then, at last, she was ready. She summoned up every ounce of courage in her body and grabbed the handle. Turning it slowly, and pushing the heavy door open in front of her, she stepped into the hallway.

Example 2: Action (fast pace)
Jane ran to the door. She grasped the handle and turned it. Pushing the door open, she moved inside. She sped down the hallway and reached the room at the far end. No one there. She turned and ran in the opposite direction.

Brainstorming

The brainstorm (also known as the spidergram or scattergram) has become ubiquitous in schools, and with very good reason. It has a whole range of uses within the classroom, including:

- As an excellent way of gathering ideas together.
- For whole-class session when first introducing a new topic.
- Imposing an initial structure on our thoughts and ideas.
- Helping to develop lateral thinking by the use of arrows which create a series of sections and subsections.

Our students are encouraged to use brainstorming in many different areas of the curriculum. Because brainstorms are so commonly used, it's worth thinking up some new approaches so that we keep our use of the technique effective, fresh and interesting. Here are some ideas about how you might do this.

- *Use colours*: The use of colours helps to segregate the ideas into different areas, and also makes the brainstorm more visually appealing. For instance, when creating a brainstorm on 'Our World' as a geography topic, you might use blue chalk or pens for water-related ideas, green for ideas connected to plants, brown for the land, and so on.
- *Make the brainstorm big!*: Big (or preferably huge) words and images are particularly appealing to children. You could take your class into the hall, or another open space, to create an enormous brainstorm on your topic. The most important words or ideas could be written in the biggest text, with those coming off them slightly smaller, radiating out from the centre of the brainstorm.
- *Make the brainstorm active*: An active approach to brainstorm-ing will also be very appealing. You might divide your class into groups and take them into the playground. Each group could be given some chalk and asked to brainstorm on the playground floor, preferably as big as possible. The class might create a playground brainstorm working together, putting a key word in the centre of the space, and giving each group an area of the topic/playground to work on.
- *Use images*: The word 'brainstorm' brings a striking picture to mind. Why not create a worksheet for individual brainstorms with a picture of an exploding brain at its centre? You could talk with your students about how the brainstorm is literally an explosion of the contents of their brain onto paper. (This gruesome idea is likely to appeal to them!)
- *Use a tight focus*: As well as gathering ideas on a topic together, brainstorms can also be used with a tighter focus. For instance, you might brainstorm all the vocabulary connected to a single word (such as 'cat') in order to write some poetry.

Researching

Once they have established what they already know, your students need to decide what other information or facts are required before they can work on their piece of writing. This might mean reading some children's story books to explore their use of language, before writing a children's book of their own. It could be a matter of identifying quotations to use in an essay on *Macbeth*. It might be a complex task such as researching an entirely new topic in depth. There are various potential sources for your children's research.

- *Texts*: I have used the word 'texts' rather than 'books' here, because some of the most useful and accessible textual information will be found in magazines and newspapers. Before researching with texts, it's a good idea to look at how these can be used most effectively. For instance, you might look at contents pages and indexes. You may also want to look at how to scan texts and take notes (see Chapter 6 for some tips on this).
- *ICT*: Teachers can now draw on a range of ICT resources: for research the most useful of these will be CD-Roms and the internet. The internet is a hugely useful tool for research, although it is surprisingly hard to use it effectively without consuming vast amounts of time. There is just so much material out there, that it is easy to find yourself moving laterally from the original point of your research, although this is not necessarily a bad thing. A good search engine is crucial: I particularly like Google for its simplicity and the relevance of its search results.
- *People*: Interviewing an 'expert' can provide very valuable and interesting research material. For instance, to research a piece of writing about their family history, your children might interview grandparents, aunts, uncles, etc. If one of your children knows an expert in a field that you are studying, you could invite him or her in to give a talk. Alternatively, your children could write letters or emails to authorities on the relevant topic.
- *Trips*: For many children, a class trip is one of the most exciting and interesting events of the school year. They

welcome the chance to get out of school for a few hours, or even a whole day. A trip also offers a chance to find fresh perspectives on a topic you are studying, and may inspire some excellent writing.

When researching, and particularly when using the internet, it is very tempting to go off at a tangent when you find some facts or information that interest you. It could be that you have plenty of time and are happy for the research to proceed in this way. However, teachers often need to get through written tasks (and the curriculum) as quickly as possible in order to fit everything in. There are various ways in which you can help students research efficiently, making effective use of class time.

- *Identify the information that is needed*: Ask your students to create a list of questions that they need or want answered. Their research can then focus on answering these questions, perhaps aiming to answer a specific number of questions in a single lesson.
- *Provide focused research material*: If you are researching in the library, liase with the librarian before the lesson. She will help you find the texts that are most likely to be useful to the children. These could then be presented on a 'research table' for the children to explore. Alternatively, for internet research you could give your students a list of the best or most useful websites.
- *Keep them 'on task'*: Going off task can be a problem, especially when using the internet, with all its temptations, and if you have a class with challenging behaviour. To keep your children 'on task', set them targets for their research. For instance, after fifteen minutes you might stop the class and ask one or two students to talk about what they have discovered. Alternatively, give each child a worksheet to complete, identifying what was discovered during the lesson, and where it was found. This would prove a useful way of collating whole-class information on a single topic.
- *Set research as a homework task*: The beauty of this approach, particularly with a large project, is that your children will naturally differentiate their learning. The more able or

enthusiastic child will seize the opportunity to delve deeply into a subject that he enjoys. For the less able or less well motivated, try to ensure that the topic being researched is something that particularly captivates their interest, or provide them with a well-targeted set of homework questions.

Mind-mapping

The mind-map is the brainstorm's 'big brother', and if you haven't already used this technique, then do give it a try. While the brainstorm gives us an effective way of noting initial ideas or information, the mind-map offers a wonderful method of organizing these points before we start to write. Mind-maps are useful for a whole range of reasons:

- They can be used to give a structured overview of data or information that you already have, or to brainstorm initial thoughts on a particular topic.
- They help give structure to complex ideas, those that are too difficult or diverse to keep in your head at one time.
- They allow you to include information that has only a lateral connection to the main topic, exploring different tangents and connections that might not be apparent at first glance.
- They work in much the same way that our brains work: we store huge amounts of information in our brains by making connections between different facts, ideas, and so on.
- They can be used across the range of curriculum subjects, and for a huge variety of different topics.

As with the brainstorm, the use of colours can help you create an effective mind-map, especially if these colours are linked to the topic and sub-topics being studied. Perhaps the best way to understand the mind-map is to look at an example. The mind-map pictured in Figure 3.1 is based on the question: 'What role does technology play in your life?'

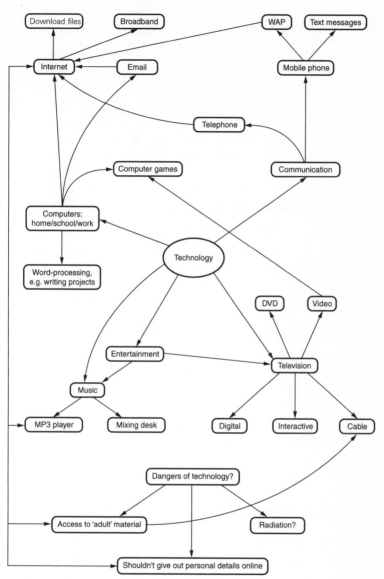

Figure 3.1 Mind-map: '*What role does technology play in your life?*'

Selecting material

Deciding what to include, and what to leave out, can be a real challenge when we are writing. This can be especially so when our students are working under exam conditions. They are so keen to include everything they know that they fail to answer the question and will often run out of time. The selection of suitable material is a vital skill to learn and practise. Selecting the appropriate material depends a great deal on the purpose of the writing: is it to answer a specific exam question, to study a topic in detail, to entertain, to inform? Here are some ideas to help you teach your children about selecting material.

- *Identify the purpose of the writing*: Take the time to discuss this with the children: talk about why they are writing on this particular topic, and what their audience will expect. The following questions will help guide your discussion.
  - Is the writing a brief summary, or an in-depth study?
  - Are you trying to entertain or inform the audience?
  - What does the reader most need or want to know?
  - Is the purpose simply to answer the exam question in a way that gains as many marks as possible?
  - If this is the case, what will the examiner want to see included?
- *Answer the question*: To succeed in their exams, your students will need to answer exam questions as accurately and concisely as possible, including just the right amount of information and material to gain maximum marks. There are lots of tips about how to do this in Chapter 4 (Essay writing) and Chapter 8 (Writing and assessment).
- *Make it interesting*: A successful piece of writing, whether fiction or non-fiction, must gain the interest of its reader. For example, in a piece of fictional writing, where there is no 'right' or 'wrong' answer, your children must learn to include what will be of most interest to the audience. They need to learn the skill of gripping the reader, finding interesting vocabulary and inventing exciting events. You can find lots of ideas about effective creative writing in Chapter 5.
- *Include something unusual*: Given 30 pieces of writing on the

same topic, it is the one with a touch of originality that will stick in the examiner's mind. This might mean the writer who expresses herself with a dash of style, who includes an unusual (but relevant) fact or detail, or who demonstrates the ability to think laterally around a subject. Bear in mind that there is a fine balance between a telling detail and the irrelevant fact included only to shock.

Planning

Many students find it hard to understand why they should plan their writing, rather than plunging straight into it. In lessons, we might help them plan their work with a whole-class introduction to the lesson, during which we identify what should be included in their writing. In exams, though, students often seem fearful of 'giving up' the amount of time that a plan would take them to write. However, a good plan is absolutely crucial to an effective piece of writing, and will save time in the long run. A well-thought-out plan has many benefits, particularly in an exam:

- It gives a clear structure to a piece of writing.
- It helps the student stay on track when answering a question.
- It ensures that everything of relevance is included.
- It helps stave off panic if the student's mind suddenly goes blank halfway through an answer.
- If there isn't time to finish the answer, it allows the examiner to see the points that would have been included.

When planning for an extended piece of writing, I would advise using a series of brainstorms, one for each paragraph or part of the work. This method is useful because:

- It encourages your students to structure and paragraph their writing correctly.
- It is a time-efficient method of planning.
- It allows the overall planning of the writing as a whole.
- The student can go back and add in additional ideas, quotations, facts to include, and so on.

From first draft to final draft

The pressure to cover the curriculum can lead to a situation where we get our students to 'bang out' pieces of writing one after the other, with only minimal thought given to drafting, reviewing, editing and redrafting the work. When time is short, the temptation is to have at least one quantifiable piece of writing to 'prove' that we have dealt with each subject area. We have surely all experienced the student who brings us a piece of rough writing, and claims to have 'finished' the work. However, many of the skills of effective writing are learned from the processes that take place between the first and final drafts. Here is a list of some of the skills involved in developing a draft into a final piece of writing.

Content:
- Identifying irrelevant content, repetition or 'waffle' and removing it.
- Ensuring that all important or relevant ideas or facts are included.
- Checking the accuracy of facts or statements.

Structure:
- Ordering ideas in the most logical and fluent way.
- Using paragraphs correctly and appropriately.
- Checking the overall 'shape' of the piece.
- Finding a good opening and ending.

Vocabulary:
- Cutting ambiguous words.
- Ensuring correct meaning and context.
- Choosing the best or most interesting vocabulary.
- Cutting unnecessary or boring words.
- Ensuring that the vocabulary matches the reader's ability and expectations.

Spelling:
- Checking the spelling of unfamiliar words.

- Identifying spelling errors and correcting them.

Grammar:
- Correcting grammatical errors.
- Altering word order or sentence structure to make the piece 'read better'.

Punctuation:
- Correcting punctuation errors.
- Altering sentence structure and punctuation to avoid excessive sentence length.
- Adding appropriate punctuation to indicate tone of voice.

Tone:
- Correcting slips from formal to informal language.
- Maintaining a constant tone throughout.
- Not patronizing the reader.

Style:
- Appealing to the identified audience.
- Using the appropriate style for the chosen form.
- Developing an interesting, gripping and individual style.

Here are some ideas for developing the ability to draft and re-draft, with the steps of reviewing and editing in between.

- *Quick draft*: Ask your children to see their first attempt as a 'quick draft', setting a specific length of time to keep the writing focused. For this draft, you might encourage them to concentrate on the content, rather than worrying about the technical accuracy of their work.
- *Test draft*: Answers written under timed conditions during a test will often provide a useful first draft (for instance for a piece of coursework). When writing under test conditions, even the less well-motivated students do tend to produce a reasonable amount of work, which can then be redrafted to a higher standard.
- *Draft on the computer*: When I write my books, I use a

computer from start to finish. This allows me to make lots of changes to content and structure without hours spent rewriting in longhand. The word processor is a wonderful tool, and I would suggest that you encourage your students to do as much of their drafting as possible on computer, whether at home or in class. In addition, the computer can give us some help with proofreading our writing: highlighting incorrect spellings and identifying poor grammar. (Obviously, the fact that exams require handwriting means that we should still get our students to practise writing longhand.)

- *Read it back*: When a student brings you a 'finished' piece of work, ask her to read it back, either to you or to a partner. This will help her see the importance of redrafting to correct errors and to make the writing sound better.
- *You be teacher*: Children love being given responsibility, so get them to swap their first drafts over and 'be teacher'. You could ask them to mark, comment on or correct their partner's work. The edited first drafts can then be returned to their owners for further correction and rewriting.
- *Set a focus*: For weaker writers, it can be disheartening to redraft their work, because there are so many mistakes to correct. For these students, set a specific focus for the redraft. This could be:
  - Looking up spellings they are uncertain about.
  - Ensuring that every sentence has a full stop.
  - Dividing their work up into paragraphs.

Presenting the final draft

When that final draft is at last finished, consider how it can best be presented as a finished piece of work. Here are some thoughts on the presentation of writing.

- *Suit the presentation to the writing*: The presentation of writing depends a great deal on the type of writing and its intended audience. An essay might be neatly handwritten or carefully typed up; a more imaginative piece of writing might use a more original style of presentation.

- *Use imaginative presentation techniques*: With many pieces of writing, the form of their final presentation can be both imaginative and attractive. For an 'ancient' historical document, you might use the old favourite of staining the paper with tea or coffee, and then burning or tearing the edges slightly. For a children's book, you might get your children to create a book cover using the computer.
- *Let your children have a say*: Your class will have their own ideas about presentation, often more imaginative or interesting ones than the teacher. Let the students have an input into the finished presentation of their writing, giving them a sense of ownership of the work.
- *'Publish' the work*: Having a real audience for their writing can be hugely motivational to children. You could publish your class's final drafts, either as a class book of writing or perhaps via the internet.

Reviewing and evaluating

Finally, your children's writing will really benefit from time spent on reviewing and evaluating. This might take place as a whole-class activity, in which the students share their work and look at each other's writing. It could be an individual activity, in which students complete a worksheet asking them questions about the finished work. Asking our children to take this step, rather than viewing it as a part of marking, will save time for the teacher. More importantly, it encourages our students to look back at a completed piece of writing and consider the content, structure, use of language, punctuation, and so on. By analysing their own work in this way, we can help them learn to set targets for the development of their writing.

The review and evaluation could focus on one particular area, for instance how technically accurate the work is, or how interesting and relevant they have made the content. Alternatively, you might ask your students to look at the steps listed at the start of this chapter, and consider which areas they still need to develop, and where they have been successful.

Part 2

Writing across the Curriculum

4 Essay writing

In this chapter I deal with the subject of essay writing. Although the material here will be of most interest to secondary school teachers, there are also plenty of strategies that could be introduced to younger students on a simpler level. For many of our students, essay writing retains a mystique, a sense that there must be some 'magic' involved. This is, of course, not true. The skills and techniques used in all forms of writing *can* be learned. I give you lots of ideas here about how to make essay writing as straightforward and engaging as possible. I give a detailed explanation of the four-step essay writing technique, a strategy that is very successful in teaching essay writing to less able students.

Some basic tips

This section gives some basic tips to get you started with the area of essay writing. I have divided these up into strategies for the teacher and for the students.

Tips for the teacher

When it comes to writing essays, practise really does make perfect. It will help your students a great deal if you:

- Go through lots and lots of sample questions with your classes.
- Show them the techniques involved by articulating the process of writing as you work through these questions.
- Share as many previous exam questions as you can with your classes.
- Demonstrate the use of planning brainstorms (see p.66) for both essay writing and also revision purposes.

- Go through the marking criteria to show them how to gain maximum marks in an exam.
- Give them examples of well-written essays, perhaps from previous students or samples that you have written yourself.
- Share the tips given in this book about different writing techniques (Chapter 3).

Bear in mind that there is no need for your students to write out a full essay every time they look at a practice question: they could simply write out a series of plans to show how they would answer the question in full in an exam.

Tips for the student

The points given below cover areas in which I have seen my own students make mistakes. These tips will need to be reiterated over and again: essay writing is a complex business and it takes time to get it right.

- *Answer the question*: Your students absolutely must learn to do this. An essay that does not answer the question that has been asked might as well not have been written at all. Right from the start, drum this point into your students.
- *Use the correct tense*: For most of the time, essays should be written in the present tense, as though describing something (for instance, an event in a novel) that is happening in the current moment. One exception to this is when recounting factual events from the past.
- *Avoid mixing tenses*: Unless it is intentional, tell your students to stick to one tense in their essays. Again, the exception to this might come in an essay where events from the past are explained, for instance in history.
- *Avoid slang*: Essays should be written in Standard English, and slang should not be used unless in direct quotation from a text.
- *Avoid abbreviations*: It is a good idea to avoid abbreviations and contractions such as 'I'd' or 'it's', because they make the essay style sound too informal.
- *Use a simple (but formal) style*: Encourage your students to use clear and simple language and expression. Although the style should be formal, discourage them from trying to sound

'posh' or using overly complicated language, as this is unnecessary and will usually backfire.

- *Don't be afraid of a personal reaction*: There will often be scope within essay questions for some type of personal comment. This might be indicated by a question that says 'Comment on your own feelings about/opinion of this ...'.

- *Give an interpretation of the evidence*: I always advise my students to suggest, rather than to insist upon the points they make. This allows scope for them to introduce unusual ideas, or to make comments about which there is some disagreement or controversy. For instance, they might start a point by saying: 'It is possible that ...' or 'One interpretation of this is ...'.

- *Take care with the 'royal we'*: Unless it is used with care, the 'royal we' can make the style of an essay seem rather pompous or self-satisfied, especially when used by younger students. There is also the danger that 'we' statements can seem overly confident, rather than interpretative (a problem if the statements are incorrect!). It is simple to minimize the use of 'we': instead of writing 'We can see that ...' your students might say 'It could be argued that ...'.

Planning an essay

When planning an essay, I would advise the use of a series of brainstorms. Each brainstorm should cover the contents of one paragraph, with perhaps four or five different points that are going to be included, and any quotations or facts that the student is planning to discuss. You can see an example of this planning method in Figure 4.1. I have based the essay plan on the very generalized question used in Chapter 3 (Figure 3.1), 'What role does technology play in your life?' Using brainstorms in this way to plan an essay has a number of advantages.

- *Time efficiency*: This method offers a quick way of giving overall structure to the piece, and consequently it is particularly useful in exams. Some students view time spent planning as 'wasted time', especially under exam conditions.

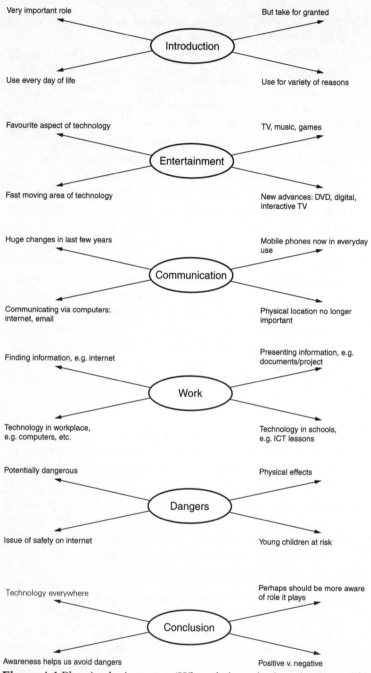

Figure 4.1 Planning brainstorms: *'What role does technology play in your life?'*

With practice your students will find that using this method for planning actually allows them to write essays more quickly and effectively.

- *Sticking to the point*: Having a single 'main idea' at the centre of each brainstorm helps your students stick to the point they are making in each paragraph.
- *Creating a structure*: Each brainstorm should provide enough material for a single paragraph. This approach will help your students remember to paragraph their essay and it will also allow them to play around with the structure of the piece before starting to write.
- *Introduction and conclusion*: It can be hard to decide exactly what you are going to say in an introduction or conclusion before the essay has actually been written. By leaving a blank brainstorm at the start and end of their plan, the students can work out the overall structure and focus of their essay, then complete the plan by filling in the introduction and conclusion brainstorms.
- *Adding in ideas*: Creating a series of brainstorms for a plan allows some flexibility if the student comes up with new ideas during the course of writing the essay. These ideas can be slotted into the overall structure by adding them to the brainstorms.
- *Demonstrating their ideas*: If a student runs out of time when writing an examination essay, the examiner may take their planning into account when marking. The brainstorm plan will give a clear indication of what the student was planning to write, had he not run out of time.

Answering the question

Do stress over and over to your students that they *must* answer the question that they've been asked. In both examination and coursework essays, they will only gain marks for answering the question, so it is vital they learn how to do this. Here are some strategies for 'answering the question' that you could share with your classes.

- *Read the questions first*: In an exam where the students are asked to comment on a piece of text, the very first thing they should do is to read the questions they will be required to answer afterwards. This should be done *before* they read the passage, as well as after. Doing this helps them focus on finding the relevant information as they read.

- *Use the question to answer the question*: This technique will help your students stick to the question, and it is also useful for those who have trouble getting started in exams. I have found it particularly helpful for Year 9 students answering their SATs exam papers. Tell your students to use the question as a statement with which to start their answer. For example, if the question asks them 'In the passage what three things does Fred hate about his school?', they could start their answer 'In the passage, Fred hates three things about his school. The first thing that he hates is …'.

- *Write out the question*: The physical action of writing out the question at the top of the page gives a strong reminder of the question your students are meant to be answering. In addition, having the question there in front of them will hopefully remind them to stick to it as they write their essay.

- *Make a plan*: A well-thought-out plan will help your students structure their essays and also to stick to the question. The plan is made with the question fresh in the mind, and it helps keep the student 'on track'.

- *Keep referring back*: It is easy to become sidetracked when writing a long essay. Encourage your students to re-read the essay question frequently (this will hopefully be written at the top of their answer). Each time she re-reads the question, the student can make a mental check that she is still answering it. If not, she should complete that sentence or paragraph quickly and then get back to the point.

How to quote

Finding and using quotations can cause problems for students, so it's important to teach them the skill of quoting. Here are some ideas and tips for you to share with your classes.

- *Use short quotes*: Students often feel that they need to use a whole sentence or even a large chunk of text when quoting. Remind the students that the examiner will normally have access to the text that they are discussing. Consequently, they only need to include enough of a quotation to make their point, or to demonstrate the part of the text to which they are referring. A short quote of about five to fifteen words is usually adequate.

- *Find the important bit*: Teach your students to hunt out the most important part of a phrase or sentence for their quote. For instance, one of the lines from Christina Rossetti's poem *A Birthday* is 'My heart is like a singing bird'. If a student was discussing this simile, he might say 'Rossetti uses the simile "like a singing bird" ', rather than quoting the whole line. When referring to a text (especially one that is reproduced in the exam paper), it is normally safe to assume that the examiner is able to read it too.

- *Have a bank of quotes*: Encourage your students to find a bank of quotes that could be used in exams and coursework essays. These quotes should cover a range of issues (for instance themes, characters, imagery in a novel) and if possible be easily accessible (perhaps written in the front of their text, if this is allowed).

- *Don't say 'I quote'*: The use of this phrase can jar in an essay, and could well lose marks for your students. Encourage them instead to say 'The author says ...' or 'The character says ...'.

The 'four-step' essay writing technique

As both an English teacher and a writer, it occurred to me that it must be possible to offer a technique for writing essays: one that would enable the less skilled to succeed in what can be a difficult writing task. The four-step technique that I came up with is one that I have developed over years of teaching students to write. By breaking down some of my own essays into their constituent parts, I was able to identify the subconscious strategies I had used to construct these extended pieces of writing.

The magic of this technique lies in its simplicity. If a student is willing to follow one step with the next in a logical way, then she will succeed in writing an essay. This technique has worked for me with weak and poorly motivated students, as well as with borderline C/D GCSE candidates, and also with those working at A/A★ standard. It has proved useful when introducing essay writing for the first time with students in Key Stage Three. There is no reason why it should not also work on a more basic level with junior school children, as an early introduction to essay writing techniques.

The technique involves four steps, each of which provides the student with one or two sentences. Put together, these sentences then create a single paragraph of the essay. The steps are repeated until the essay is finished. I developed this technique for writing English essays, but it is equally applicable to essays in other areas of the curriculum where essays are required.

The quality of the finished essay will depend on the student's grasp of the ideas or facts that he is writing about, and on his ability to express himself. The four-step technique helps keep students on track when answering an essay question. It also gives the less able a chance to write a reasonable essay of their own.

The four steps are as follows:

1. *Statement*: State something that is true, or make a comment on the subject.
2. *Evidence*: Give evidence or factual detail to support your initial statement.
3. *Explain*: Explain how the evidence links to your initial statement.
4. *Develop*: Develop your ideas, elaborating more fully, or finding a further link.

For weaker students, the fourth step can be left out, and the resulting essay will still be good enough to gain a reasonable grade in an exam or a piece of coursework. Here are two examples of the four-step technique in action. To show that this technique is applicable across the curriculum, my examples relate to English literature and science.

Example 1

1. *Statement:* In *Romeo and Juliet*, Shakespeare makes much use of imagery connected to light.
2. *Evidence:* While Romeo waits below Juliet's balcony, he tells us 'The brightness of her cheek would shame those stars,/As daylight doth a lamp.'
3. *Explain:* Here Romeo uses his words to paint a picture that is saturated with images of light. Just as the daylight is brighter than a lamp, so Romeo feels that Juliet's beauty is so radiant, it would 'shame' even the stars.
4. *Develop:* These images of light contrast strongly with images of darkness, and of the night, particularly at the end of the play, when the lovers die together in a dark tomb.

Here's the full paragraph, as it might appear in an essay:

In *Romeo and Juliet*, Shakespeare makes much use of imagery connected to light. While Romeo waits below Juliet's balcony, he tells us 'The brightness of her cheek would shame those stars,/As daylight doth a lamp.' Here Romeo uses his words to paint a picture that is saturated with images of light. Just as the daylight is brighter than a lamp, so Romeo feels that Juliet's beauty is so radiant, it would 'shame' even the stars. These images of light contrast strongly with images of darkness, and of the night, particularly at the end of the play, when the lovers die together in a dark tomb.

Example 2

1. *Statement:* Animals with a backbone (vertebrates) are divided into five classes, and these classes of vertebrate are linked by evolution.
2. *Evidence:* The five classes, in order of evolution, are fish, amphibians, reptiles, birds and mammals.
3. *Explain:* The first vertebrates were fish, and from these came the amphibians. The amphibians gave rise to reptiles, which eventually evolved into both birds and mammals.
4. *Develop:* These five classes of vertebrates are divided into cold-blooded creatures (fish, amphibians and reptiles) and warm-blooded animals (birds and mammals).

Again, here's the full paragraph, as it would appear in an essay on this subject:

> Animals with a backbone (vertebrates) are divided into five classes, and these classes of vertebrate are linked by evolution. The five classes, in order of evolution, are fish, amphibians, reptiles, birds and mammals. The first vertebrates were fish, and from these came the amphibians. The amphibians gave rise to reptiles, which eventually evolved into both birds and mammals. These five classes of vertebrates are divided into cold-blooded (fish, amphibians and reptiles) and warm-blooded (birds and mammals).

Now let's consider each step in more detail.

Writing the statement

Depending on the curriculum area, and the subject of the essay, the statement might be something that is actually true (i.e. an accepted fact), or a comment that the student believes to be true (i.e. an interpretation). Encourage your students to couch any facts that they are unsure about as a possibility, supposition or interpretation, suggesting that something might be true, rather than stating it as an absolute fact.

Finding the evidence

The evidence to support the statement may take various forms. Encourage your students to experiment with using each of these approaches.

- *Factual detail*: In some subjects and topics there will be factual details for students to use. These facts stretch across the curriculum and include generally accepted terminology, as well as 'true facts' such as a person's date of birth or when one country invaded another.
- *Quotation*: Quotes may take the form of a line, phrase or sentence from a text that illustrates the statement. They might also be a quote from a textbook in which the author makes a statement that supports the initial contention.

- *Events*: Your students might describe an event to support their statement. For instance, in an English essay they might use something that happens in the story to illustrate a character's personality. Alternatively, in a history essay, the event described could be an actual historical incident related to the original statement.

Explaining the link

The third step involves exploring the link between the initial statement and the evidence that has been given. The ability to make these links between comment, and evidence for that comment, is one of the most important skills in essay writing. Exploring or explaining the link forces the student to ensure that the initial statement has been well thought-out, and that the evidence given does actually support the statement that has been made.

Exploring the link might be a simple explanation of how the quote or evidence does actually support the statement that has been made. For instance, in the *Romeo and Juliet* example above, the writer notes that the picture Romeo paints with his words is 'saturated with light'. Explaining the link can also involve a development of both the statement and the evidence. For instance, in the same example, the writer goes on to explain exactly how the light-based image itself actually works.

Developing the point

The fourth step – development – is the hardest for students to grasp. However, the first three steps will still provide them with a reasonable essay. The fourth step is the difference between a student who might achieve a grade D–F at GCSE, and a student who is capable of achieving a grade A–C. Development of a point might take place in one of the following ways.

- *Further explanation*: Development might involve a further indication of ways in which the evidence supports the initial comment.
- *Links to other areas within the topic or text*: It might also be about finding a link to another area of the subject being explored. For instance, when writing about a fictional text, students

might explain how their point relates to other events or significant factors within the text.

- *A connection to the social or historical context*: The development could be the student making a connection to the wider context of the subject being discussed. For example, when writing about the theme of the supernatural in *Macbeth*, the point might be developed by discussing the historical context in which the play was written, and the attitudes to witchcraft at this time.
- *A lateral connection*: The development could also be the student making a lateral connection to another idea or area within the topic. This could mean a student writing about an author's characterization linking the characters in a text to influential people in the author's life.
- *A wider issue*: Similarly, the development could involve suggesting or explaining a link to a wider issue within the topic. So a student writing about the environment within a science essay might link the points made to the current global environmental situation.

Introductions and conclusions

Writing introductions and conclusions is a surprisingly hard skill to master. Some students find it very hard to start an essay, and end up taking a long time to write only a poor standard of introduction. Part of the problem is that the introduction to an extended piece of writing is often best done *after* the body of the writing has been finished. This is fine in a coursework essay, which can be drafted and redrafted, perhaps on a computer, but it is impossible to do in an examination situation. The tips below will help your students understand more about the process of writing introductions and conclusions.

- *Give a taste of what is to come*: The best introductions give a flavour of the essay to come, a general taster of the points that will be made. The best writers will find a way to hint at what is to come, both in the things that they say and also in the language they use.
- *Use the question to start the essay*: A good way for weaker

students to start an introduction is to turn the question that has been asked into the opening statement. This is especially helpful for those who have difficulty getting their essays underway. If the question asks 'What factors led to the start of the Second World War?' the student could begin the essay by saying 'There were a number of factors which led to the outbreak of the Second World War.'

- *Use the introduction to introduce the subject*: This point might seem obvious, but it is often ignored. The aim is to give an introduction to the writer's viewpoint on the question that has been asked.

- *Find a lateral point to make*: In the example given below of an essay introduction, the point made about the language of movement is actually relatively peripheral to the overall essay content. However, it provides an interesting and engaging way into the subject for the writer and the reader.

- *Use the conclusion to summarize the content*: The conclusion should provide an overall, general summary of what has been discussed in the essay, summing up the points that have been made. Encourage your students to come to some sort of conclusion, especially if the essay question has asked for specific comment on a topic. For instance, in answer to a question asking 'Which of these two characters do you most sympathize with?' the student should include a summary of the opinions they have given and come to a definitive answer to the question asked.

- *Don't be afraid of the personal*: In the example below, you will see that the essay ends on a highly personal note. Giving an individual view or comment on a subject can be a strong way of concluding an essay, especially one that is about a subject of importance to the writer.

- *Don't be afraid of the emotional*: Similarly, if it is relevant to the subject under discussion (for instance in an interpretive piece of writing, or one that analyses a fictional text), a strong conclusion will often involve the declaration of an emotional response to the subject.

- *Avoid direct reference to the content*: When unsure of what to write, students sometimes make the introduction a list of what will be in the essay, and the conclusion a list of what has just been said. This will read in a very pedestrian style, and will not gain them any marks.

Perhaps the best way to illustrate the points above is to look at an example of an introduction and a conclusion.

Essay question: Discuss the role that dance should play within schools, considering its strengths and weaknesses as part of an increasingly crowded curriculum. What problems must be solved if dance is to play a full and valuable role in the educational experience?

Introduction
People use the language of movement when an experience touches them deeply – we might say 'I am walking on air' or 'my heart leapt'. These instinctive metaphors give us an insight into the fundamental role that movement plays in our lives. It is understandable that teachers neglect dance and movement: burdened with a heavy workload and a lack of experience in this area, there are other issues that probably seem more pressing. However, I feel it is vital to challenge the attitude that sport alone is adequate to satisfy our children's physical needs. There are so many educational possibilities inherent within movement lessons – dance helps us to develop not only our physical skills, but also our imaginative and creative abilities.

Conclusion
Dance has been a part of my life for twenty years. The expression and insight that it has given me have been instrumental in the development of my character. Dance allows us to express ourselves imaginatively and creatively. It also provides a wonderful opportunity for physical activity. If teachers can provide opportunities for their children to experience the richness inherent in movement and dance activities, I believe they will find its value and importance priceless in their students' education.

Essay writing with the most able

Writing essays offers an excellent way to stretch the writing skills of your most able students. Through the medium of an essay, these students might explore different ways of structuring their work, or look at using linguistic techniques to give their writing more interest. Here are some strategies for working on essay writing with your strongest students.

- *Develop the use of tone*: The best essays use a writing style that reflects the tone of their subject. If a student is writing about a piece of text with a sad, emotional theme, this could be reflected in the choice of words and style of the essay.
- *Develop the use of language devices*: Language devices can be used within essays in any subject area. For instance, the writer might use repetition to link together a series of ideas over several paragraphs. He could use a metaphor to deepen an explanation or alliteration to make the writing sound more appealing. He might use the technique of 'listing in threes', in which three points are listed in turn, building in power and emphasis each time.
- *Develop the use of pace*: Pacing a piece of writing is a subtle skill. Your most able students could experiment with altering word or sentence length, and adding or taking away punctuation, to vary the pace of the writing within an essay.
- *Develop 'a voice'*: The best essays give the reader a sense of the writer's 'voice'. A satirical essayist might use a cynical tone, a more emotional essay writer could use a passionate voice. Maintaining a consistent 'voice' throughout an essay will make the writing far more appealing to the reader.
- *Give the reader something to chew on*: An essay that includes a surprise fact or comment, or that concludes by leaving a question hanging in the air, can be very powerful. Encourage the most polished essay writers among your students to make their essays striking for the reader.

5 Creative writing

Creative writing can be used right across the school curriculum. Although stories, scripts and poems have traditionally been forms used within the English lesson, they actually provide a useful way into writing in many different subjects. Creative writing appeals strongly to children – they welcome the chance to use their imagination, to invent new people or imagine new storylines. The children we teach are surrounded by creative writing outside school, through the whole range of the media. In this chapter you will find lots of information, tips and advice about developing the myriad skills and techniques involved in creative writing.

Creating a fiction

As teachers, we spend much of our time creating 'fictions' for our students. For instance, a teacher who uses the 'strict and scary' model described in my book *Getting the Buggers to Behave* (London: Continuum, 2002), is creating a fiction about herself as a teacher. Few of us are actually 'strict and scary' people in our lives outside school. A teacher who uses this model in her professional life is unlikely to shout at or be 'scary' with her friends and family. However, she might find that by creating this fiction about herself within school she gets better behaviour from her students.

Our children, too, are complicit in the fictions we create. In fact, schools are reliant on the students' willingness to go along with these fictions to maintain a sense of order and control. There is no real reason why children should behave for and obey their teachers but, in the majority of cases, they do. Children love being part of a fiction, and as teachers we can utilize this to engage with and motivate our students in their writing. Using creative writing in the classroom allows us to tap into this enjoyment as a way of getting better work from our students.

The importance of genre

One of the best ways into any piece of writing for the teacher is via genre, and this applies especially to creative writing. Genre is a French word that literally means 'type'. The children of the twenty-first century are positively steeped in genre: through the movies they watch, the books they read, the television programmes they see and the computer games they play. Certain genres really capture the children's attention, for instance science fiction, crime, horror. The Harry Potter phenomenon has seen an upsurge of interest in magic. Popular television programmes such as *Buffy the Vampire Slayer* have reinforced this fascination. By approaching creative writing via genre, we can spark our students' interest and get them motivated in their work.

The elements of genre

Asking our children to write within a genre gives us a wonderful chance to exercise their writing skills. They must select the correct elements to include: the right types of character, the likely locations, the appropriate words and terminology. They must also think carefully about audience expectations when writing within a specific genre. Generally speaking, genres follow set rules, although many of the best genre stories either break or subvert these rules in some way. A story in the magic genre is almost honour-bound to feature witches and wizards, while a story in the crime genre is going to feature a criminal, a victim and a detective at the very least. The list below gives an outline of the typical elements of genre.

- Characters
- Location
- Storyline
- 'Lighting' and atmosphere
- 'Props' (objects)
- Costume or clothing
- Type of dialogue

- Likely vocabulary
- Plot events or features

When first introducing the subject, a useful exercise is to ask your students to pick one genre, and list the 'standard elements' that they would expect to find. For instance, in a crime story, you might have the following features:

- *Characters*: victim, criminal, 'scapegoat', witnesses, detective, police officers.
- *Location*: back alley, police station, bank, getaway car.
- *Storyline*: a crime takes place; the police work to solve it; the criminal is caught.
- *'Lighting' and atmosphere*: dark, foggy streets; tense, scary atmosphere.
- *'Props'*: weapons, handcuffs, evidence, photofit posters.
- *Costume or clothing*: police uniforms, a blood-stained shirt, prison uniforms.
- *Type of dialogue*: formal language used by police, criminals might use slang.
- *Likely vocabulary*: crime, criminal, victim, witness, forensics, fingerprints, etc.
- *Plot events or features*: the discovery of a body, the clue that is a 'red herring'.

After creating a list of standard elements, you could give your students a selection of texts from different genres. These could be studied to identify the various elements that define the genre of each piece.

Setting an atmosphere for genre writing

The use of genres offers you a wonderful opportunity to create an atmosphere or mood in your classroom. By doing this, you will spark the children's interest, and engage their attention, inspiring them when they come to write. To create an atmosphere for genre writing in your classroom, you might use:

- Lighting effects – a blackout, candles, torches.
- Sound effects – animal noises, weather sounds.
- Objects – props and other items related to the genre.
- Costumes – for the teacher/students to wear.

- In-role work – with the teacher/students taking on characters from the genre.

Playing with genre

Playing around with genre can prove a very useful and highly motivating approach to creative writing. For example, you might start by asking your class to rewrite various genre extracts into another genre. Students seem to love subverting or adapting the original form and intentions of a piece of writing. When they do this, they are learning about and developing an understanding of the conventions of different written forms.

I experienced a wonderful example of the way that forms and genres can be played with or subverted when I was teaching my very first Year 9 class in preparation for their SATs. We had studied *Romeo and Juliet* in some detail, and we were working on the party scene, where the young lovers meet for the first time. We had also been exploring slang and dialect, discussing the language that Shakespeare used, and how his plays might sound today. I set an activity to translate the party scene into modern–day language, adding slang or using dialect as the class wished. Two of my students, who came from an Afro-Caribbean background, worked together to produce a fantastic patois version of the scene, which we performed in class. Here is an extract from their scene, showing the impressive way in which they were able to play with the original words and subvert the form in a way that I believe Shakespeare himself might have enjoyed.

Rochon and JuJu

[Enter MASTER CARLTON, MISS CAROL, JUJU, TYRONE, 'ELPER and guests.]

CARLTON: Welcome ladies and gentlemen. Which one of you lovely ladies want fi dance? If you say no a corns you a grow pon dem foot, come bus' out the tune, nam and drink until your belly bus!

[Ladies kiss their teef and look away.]

Come rest yourself cos.

CARLOS: Jesus peace a thirty years since mi last see you.
CARLTON: A nuh that long. It was at Lucil wedding.
CARLOS: Oh yes, mi remember that well. That was in the old days when we were young and lively.
CARLTON: Those were the days man!
ROCHON: Who's that pretty woman over deh so?
SERVANT 1: Mi nuh know sir.
ROCHON: She kinda nice you know. We warn fi teck her to mi yard tonight. Mi just go teck a little breeze over deh so.

Here are some more ideas about how you could subvert or play with genre in your classroom.

- *Subverting audience expectations*: When we read a story, we do so with certain expectations about what will happen and how the characters will behave within that genre. This is especially so with the genre of fairy tales: these stories have simple, traditional plots, and use highly stereotyped characters. By subverting audience expectations, writers can create some wonderful and humorous effects. For instance, the author Babette Cole confounds audience expectations by rewriting Cinderella as *Prince Cinders*.
- *Changing the form*: Changing the form in which a story is presented can produce some interesting and often hilarious results. For instance, you might rewrite and perform the story of *The Three Little Pigs*:
  - As a football match report.
  - As a TV news story.
  - As a 'Jerry Springer'-style chat show.
  - As an opera.
  - As a soap opera.
- *Updating and changing the language*: In the *Romeo and Juliet* example above, the language has been updated and changed into patois, while still retaining the meaning of the original. Other ideas for updating and changing language might include a Victorian melodrama rewritten in the style of 'Ali G', or conversely a modern-day crime story rewritten in the style of Jane Austen.

- *Changing the perspective*: Certain genres tend to use specific perspectives. The crime story is often written from the viewpoint of the detective, or the thriller from the perspective of the hero. By shifting the perspective you can achieve some very interesting results. For instance, in the hilarious 'Dr Xargle' books, the writers view Earth and Earthlings from the perspective of visiting aliens.

Finding inspiration

Finding inspiration for writing might be about discovering the initial spark for a story, or about choosing ways to develop a piece of descriptive writing more fully. Inspiration comes in many shapes and forms: here are some suggestions to help you find it.

- *Starting points*: Give your children some 'starting points' for their fiction to help inspire them to create a story. You might give them a character, an emotion, a place and an item from which to develop their writing, for instance:
  - King / angry / haunted house / spell book.
  - Dog / lonely / castle / key.
  - Astronaut / terrified / alien planet / spaceship.
- *Props*: Children love having an actual item to work with, especially something that seems out of place in the classroom. With props we take them outside of their ordinary lives and into a fiction where the imagination can roam freely. Working with a prop might lead to ideas for a character, a place, an event. It is useful to have a box of different props in your classroom to help whenever inspiration is needed. In this box you might have different types of bags and purses, some jewellery boxes, feathers, stones, money from different countries, and so on.
- *Associations*: Inspiration can be found by making associations between one thing and another. For instance, you might bring an exotic piece of fruit into the classroom and ask the children what sort of places they associate with it. You could discuss associations between a certain smell or sound and a particular place. For example, what smells do the children associate with a hospital, or with a shopping centre? What sounds do they associate with a zoo, or with an airport?

- *Bag of words*: When approaching a piece of creative writing, it is a great idea to have a bag of words that your children can dip into. The words in this bag should be unusual, ones that stimulate the imagination. You could even have a selection of bags, one for places, one for characters, one for types of weather, and so on.
- *Music*: Listening to a piece of music can inspire your children's imagination, and make them think of different moods, places, people, etc. By starting a writing lesson listening to music, your students should also become more focused for their work.
- *Take them into the world of the imagination*: For this exercise, ask your children to close their eyes (they could do this lying on the floor in a comfortable position). Now move them into an imaginary world, by taking them on a 'journey'. Your journey could be to a desert island, into an enchanted forest, into outer space, anywhere really. Give them a brief description of their journey and what they see, but do not be too specific – let their imaginations fill in the details.

Using your senses

Most of us naturally use our sight and hearing when we are writing creatively, but of course we also have the chance to explore taste, touch and smell. Here are some ideas to get your children using their senses more fully in their written work.

- *Senses worksheet*: This approach is useful for brainstorming vocabulary before writing a poem or story and it can also be used for other areas of the curriculum (for instance looking at the impact pollution has on people through their sensory responses to it). Draw up a worksheet on which each of the senses has one column: see, hear, taste, touch and smell. The children then brainstorm words connected to the topic, under the headings of each of their senses.
- *Removing one sense*: Depriving your children of one of their senses encourages them to use their other senses more fully. You might remove the sense of sight by using a blindfold, then give a variety of objects for your students to touch,

smell, listen to and even taste. You could remove the sense of touch, by asking your children to put their hands behind their backs, then describing how different objects would feel without actually touching them.

- *Colours*: This is a fun exercise I did when I was at school (and have remembered ever since, which proves it was highly engaging). You may be sceptical about it, but do give it a try. It provides an excellent way into writing work about colours, and also creates a strong sense of focus in the classroom. The student is blindfolded, and then a sheet of coloured paper is put in front of him. Ask him to touch the paper and focus very hard on 'feeling' the colour. Although it may be only a matter of luck, when I did this exercise at school there were certain people in my class who could 'feel' the colours correctly most of the time.

- *Weather*: Ask your children to shut their eyes and imagine a particular type of weather (you specify this), for instance a storm. Now ask them to move through their senses, one at a time, as you say them. What can they see? What can they hear? This work can lead to some excellent descriptive writing. It also encourages the children to empathize with their characters, feeling what a character might feel if she was stuck outside during a storm, or trapped on a desert island in the heat.

- *Place and sound*: For this exercise, the whole class is involved in creating a place by using sound. Get your class lying in a circle on the floor, with their feet facing out of the circle and their heads nearly touching. In this way, they each get the best possible effect. The teacher specifies a place for the children to create through sound, for instance a prison building up to a riot, a ship in a storm, a haunted house on a windy night, a Victorian asylum, and so on. The children should start quietly, adding sounds as and when they feel it is appropriate (not everyone has to make a sound at once). The sound effects build up to a climax, before ending, either by fading out, or by stopping abruptly. Preferably the class should decide as a whole (without any signal) when it is a good point to fade out or stop the soundtrack. You may find at first that your children are too noisy, or that they do not work well together. However, with practice, you will find that the 'places' created can be extraordinarily powerful and inspirational. You might also tape this exercise, either to play back to your children, or to use as a 'mood' tape for writing.

Writing fiction

Fiction writing allows us to work in the realm of the imagination, and let our minds run free. Although writing a story just to learn about writing a story is a task for English lessons, there are many other areas where writing fiction can prove extremely useful. Fiction writing can give children a wonderful outlet for their worries and emotions, offering a pretend world in which they can explore those issues which they find troubling. For this reason, it might be used to very good effect in a PSHE lesson. The following sections deal with the techniques involved in story writing: much that is covered here will also be applicable to writing scripts.

Creating characters

One of the most exciting things about writing fiction is the chance to create imaginary people, and even creatures, all of our very own. At first, many writers have a tendency to write about the people they know. Constant exposure to television and film might also mean that your writers fall back on copying plots and characters they have seen on screen. Here are a range of ideas for encouraging your students to create interesting and believable characters of their own.

- *Props*: Props can be an excellent way of developing interesting characters. You might bring a piece of clothing into the classroom and ask the children to talk about the different characters who might wear it. Similarly, you might 'find' the bag that belongs to a character (perhaps at the scene of a crime), and look at the contents of the bag to decide the type of person who owns it.
- *What's in a name?*: Give your children some unusual names, and ask them to write about the characters that they visualize. Choose a name that has additional layers of

meaning or in which the words hint at the character's personality, such as 'Cruella de Ville'.

- *Setting the scene*: Set up a 'scene' in your classroom, which the characters have just left. To give an example that I have used myself, you might put:
  - Two hands of cards on a table.
  - Some coins scattered across the table and onto the floor.
  - Two chairs (one upright, the other overturned).
  - An empty glass.
  - A bottle that has fallen to the floor.

  Now talk with your children about what has just happened in this scene, and what sort of characters might be in this story. You could ask your students to act out the scene that took place. This type of work can lead to some really inspired story or scriptwriting.

- *Hot seating*: This drama technique is excellent for developing characters, and is loved by children of all ages. It also works well for questioning characters in a text you are studying, whether a GCSE text or a book for young children. Ask for a volunteer to sit in the 'hot seat', facing the rest of the class. This volunteer is going to play a character. The character could be invented beforehand, but it is often best to let him or her take shape as you go along. You can do this by asking questions that force the person in the 'hot seat' to invent the story of this character on the spot. For instance, the teacher might start by saying 'I understand that you were seen running away from the Royal Oak Public House, covered in blood? Can you tell me what you had to do with the murder of Fred Bloggs?' The character in the 'hot seat' must then respond to this and the following questions.

- *The 'Judgement Chair'*: This is another drama technique that will help invent rounded and interesting characters. Again, it can be used for questioning characters that already exist in a text you are studying. It could also be used to study citizenship topics or PSHE issues such as teenage pregnancy or drug abuse. A volunteer sits in the 'Judgement Chair', and then various other characters from that person's life come up to pass judgement. The volunteer may respond in role to the judgements, or might simply listen to what is said. For instance, you might use the scenario of a child who has been caught shoplifting. The characters judging the child could include her parents, brothers and sisters, police officers, teachers, etc. The parents might come up to her and say 'How could you do this to us? We're so disappointed in you ...'.

- *What do I need to know?*: Encourage your children to invent lots of background information for the people they make up. This information could come under various categories, for instance physical, social, psychological, and emotional. Some of the things they might need to know include:
  - What the character looks like.
  - What he wears.
  - Who his parents are.
  - What he does.
  - What makes him angry?
  - What makes him happy?
  - What he likes to spend money on, etc.

  Your students could create a factsheet for their character, or they could write an interview (perhaps with a partner asking the questions).

Show, don't tell

A classic mistake that many writers make in their fiction is to *tell* the reader what is happening, rather than *showing* them. This is usually how young children first write their stories: 'Anna was sad, she was sad because she lost her teddy', and so on. Showing rather than telling is important for several reasons.

- *Maintaining the illusion*: The ideal in our writing is for there to be nothing that intrudes between the reader and what he is reading, nothing that 'breaks the spell' of the text. When the writer *tells* the reader what is happening in her story, this creates an authorial intrusion that lessens the strength of the text. Instead of allowing the reader to work things out for himself, the writer feels the need to explain what her characters are thinking and feeling. A writer who is 'telling' might say 'Shami was really angry'. A writer who is 'showing' might say 'Shami clenched her fists and a dark look came over her face.'

- *Encouraging empathy*: Showing invites the reader to step into the character's shoes, to empathize totally with them, perhaps even 'becoming' that person while he or she is reading. It is this empathy that we are talking about when we say we became 'lost' in a book, that it was so engrossing that we forgot all about the real world.

- *Treating the reader right*: By showing rather than telling, the writer also makes an assumption about his or her readers – that they are intelligent and interested enough to work out the characters' emotions for themselves, rather than needing to be held by the hand and told.

- *Quality of writing*: Showing encourages a more visual, detailed writing style, because the writer is forced to describe the characters and what they do in detail, rather than using blunt phrases such as 'she was sad/angry/happy'. It also tends to create a style with more energy and pace, rather than a series of plodding 'facts', as you will see in the examples given below.

- *Quality of characterization*: Similarly, the writer is encouraged to create more realistic, believable characters. The student has to work out how the character might behave if she were angry, what mannerisms or actions she might use, and so on.

If we think about the way in which the best stories work, it is because the reader can visualize the people and events in his or her imagination. We see the story happening before our eyes, and this allows us to empathize with the characters, drawing us into the story. So, we have no need for the author to tell us what the characters are thinking and feeling – we know already, because we 'see' them in our heads. The following examples demonstrate the difference between 'telling' and 'showing' the reader.

Example 1: 'Telling' the reader
Julie was very sad. She knew that she didn't have any friends. This made her feel terrible, and she hated going to school each day. She knew that Katie and Emma hated her most of all. She felt like hitting Emma. It was all Emma's fault, but what could Julie do about it?

Example 2: 'Showing' the reader
A tear trickled down Julie's cheek. 'I'm not going to school,' she told her mum.

'Oh yes you are,' her mum replied.

A bitter knot of resentment pulled at Julie's stomach as she tugged on her school uniform. Dashing the tears from her cheeks, she thought back to what had happened in the playground the day before.

'You're not playing with us,' Katie said, Emma standing behind her, a twisted smile on her face.

Julie clenched her fists hard, her fingernails biting into her palms, her head swimming with thoughts of revenge.

Narrative voice and viewpoint

Before writing a story, it is essential for the writer to establish where he stands in relation to his characters and his readers. There are three 'basic' narrative voices, of which the two most commonly used are explained below. With the third option, the 'omniscient viewpoint', the writer assumes a 'godlike' position, overseeing everything that happens in the story. This viewpoint can feel quite intrusive, and perhaps because of this it tends not to appeal to modern readers.

- *First-person viewpoint*: The story is told from the perspective of the first person, using 'I' as the narrative voice. The person speaking might be one of the characters in the story, or it could be the voice of the writer. This narrative voice encourages the reader to associate strongly with the character telling the story, as we see events from her perspective. However, the writer cannot include events that his narrator does not experience directly.
- *Third-person viewpoint*: The story is told from a third-person perspective, using 'she' or 'he'. Stories using a third-person narrator are usually told from the viewpoint of one character, with the writer allowing us access to the thoughts and feelings of this one person. Sometimes, however, two or more characters may be used. This viewpoint does not create such a strong sense of empathy, as the reader is not

viewing the story through the eyes of one person. However, the writer can describe events outside the direct experience of his or her characters.

Dialogue

We might think that writing dialogue should be the easiest thing in the world. After all, we spend our lives communicating through speech. Surely all we need to do is to turn our spoken words into written ones? However, there is much more to writing interesting and exciting dialogue than simply transferring speech onto the page. Here are some tips about how you can encourage your students to write imaginative and effective speech for the characters in their stories. Many of these ideas will also apply to the process of writing play scripts.

- *Conflict, conflict, conflict*: Conflict is a vital aspect in any decent piece of fiction and it is a crucial part of writing good dialogue. Having conflicts helps avoid the dreary 'what did you have for breakfast?' type of speech. Some ways that you might inject conflict into dialogue include the following:
  - *Conflicting agendas*: Where one character wants the opposite to the other, and each is fighting for her own position.
  - *Blocking*: Where one person is refusing to agree with what the other says, and is throwing up a series of complaints or issues.
  - *Conflicting personalities*: Where each character has a very different personality, for instance one person is easily angered, while the other stays calm.
- *Avoiding boredom*: Much of what we say in everyday life is entirely lacking in conflict. However, when writing a story, we need to find some way of engrossing the reader, otherwise she will simply stop reading! One useful way of avoiding boredom is to twist what might have been a normal conversation into something a little more exciting, for instance by including details specific to the characters involved. In the examples below (p.93) you will see how a mundane conversation about the time can be turned into something altogether more interesting.

- *Twisting the words*: What we say and what we mean can be two very different things. There is often a subtext going on behind our words, and this makes things more interesting for the reader. Encourage your students to play with dialogue and meaning, to have their characters saying one thing while meaning something else, or misinterpreting what the other person says.

- *Learning to listen*: Encourage your students to listen to the speech that surrounds them, for instance the conversations that they might overhear on the bus in the morning. You could set this activity as a homework task, perhaps asking them to make a note of three unusual or interesting lines of dialogue they overhear during the course of a day, and then build a story around these.

- *Thinking about character*: The way that we speak tells other people a lot about our personality, upbringing and background. For instance, an elderly gentleman who spent his life in the army would use speech very differently to a young child on her first day at school.

- *Communicating tone*: The tone of our characters' voices can be communicated in a variety of ways. Most tempting is to use a range of verbs and adverbs, such as 'he shouted' or 'he said angrily'. However, these dialogue 'tags' can become very intrusive for the reader, especially if a number of them are used within one section of dialogue. A better option is to try to make the words themselves and the way that they are structured hint at the tone of a character's voice.

- *The invisible 'said'*: The word 'said' is, to a large extent, 'invisible' to the reader, and it allows her to focus instead on the dialogue itself. It is often a much better option than more visually intrusive words such as 'replied'.

- *Removing the dialogue tags*: It is often possible to actually remove dialogue tags such as 'said' altogether, particularly if there are only two characters speaking in a scene. Once it has been established who is speaking and in what order, there is no real need for any further explanation.

Example 1: How not to write dialogue

'What time is it?' Jamie asked breathlessly.

'Half past two,' Tara answered calmly.

'It's nearly time to go back to work then,' Jamie said with a sigh.

'Do we have to?' Tara moaned plaintively.

'Yes,' Jamie answered with finality.

Example 2: How to write dialogue

Jamie glanced at his bare wrist. 'Tara, you got the time?'

'The time for what?' She winked at him and flashed a smile.

'No, what time is it?' He tapped his wrist to indicate where a watch should have been. Tara's smile vanished.

'How the hell should I know the time, Jamie? What happened to that watch I gave you for your birthday?'

'It's ...'

'Don't tell me you've broken it already, Jamie.'

'Don't start, Tara.'

'What do you mean, 'don't start'? That watch cost me a bloody fortune.'

'Why is everything about money with you, Tara?'

Setting

Fiction can take place in any setting that we choose, from the mountains of Borneo to the snowy wastes of Alaska, from the streets of London to a spaceship on a mission to Mars. Writers are often encouraged to 'write about what you know'. Although our students might not have had the opportunity to travel abroad, most of them will have had ample opportunity to see other places and lives on the television. In addition, there is of course always room for them to use their imaginations.

When you are setting up your classroom for some creative writing, you could turn one part or even your whole room into 'another place', to inspire your children. This might mean:

- Setting up a haunted house by blacking out your room and adding some spooky sound effects.

- For a story about Native American Indians, asking your class to act as a 'tribe', inventing their own tribal name and rituals, and having 'pow-wows' sitting in a circle on the floor.
- Lining up the chairs to make aeroplane seats, and then flying off somewhere new.
- Putting a 'magic carpet' on the floor, to inspire journeys to invented places.

The importance of conflict

A story without conflict is boring – if the character does not face any problems or difficulties in his fictional journey, then the reader has no reason to become involved in the story. Conflict adds tension for the reader – we become caught up in the story because we are worried for the characters, fearful that they might be in danger of some kind. Adding conflict to a story makes the difference between a dull piece of writing and an interesting one. A writer who does not utilize conflict might tell a story where Fred gets up in the morning, goes to school, comes home, does his homework and goes to bed. A writer who uses conflict might have Fred getting up in the morning and overhearing his parents having a huge quarrel, or having Fred arrive at school to find that aliens have taken over his world, and he is the only one who realizes. At once, the reader is engaged and wants an answer to the question 'what happens next?'.

Learning to include conflict in stories is one of the fundamental lessons of good fiction writing. There are three basic conflicts: person against person, person against nature, and person against him- or herself. Here are some ideas for different ways of introducing conflict, and consequently tension, into a story.

- *Problems*: Readers instinctively engage with a character who is experiencing problems of some type, because they want to know what is going to happen, and whether the character will overcome his problems. The more problems that a writer throws at a character, the higher the level of conflict and tension. These problems might be:
  - A character who has trouble making friends.
  - Someone with a medical problem that must be overcome.
  - A person who is experiencing financial problems.

- A character who faces an ethical dilemma.
- An external, physical problem, for instance a character who gets lost in a storm.
- *Obstacles*: When an obstacle stands between a character and his or her goal, this creates conflict. (For instance, the classic example of *Romeo and Juliet*, in which the obstacle that the two lovers face is the hatred between their parents.) It is important that the goal is clear – that the reader realizes what the character is striving for, and how the obstacles are preventing her from reaching her goal.
- *Between characters*: Conflict will also arise between the hero/ heroine and the villain in a story. This conflict might be apparent in the actions that they take, for instance fighting with each other, or in the dialogue between them.

Here are some specific exercises to use in your classroom when teaching your students about conflict.

- *The worst thing*: Decide on a character with the children, for instance a boy who loves to play football, or a dog who is terrified of storms. Now ask them to think of some of the worst things that could happen to that character. For the boy who loves football, it could be breaking his leg, or being given a detention that means he misses a crucial match. For the scared dog, it could be that her owners shut her outside during a storm, or that she must go out into the storm to save someone. Immediately, these scenarios offer your students conflict with which to make their stories exciting.
- *You can't have it because* ...: Conflict is created when a character is prevented from having what he or she wants. Ask your students to think of a character who really really wants something: for instance a girl who desperately wants to go out with a boy in her class, or an astronaut who desperately wants to fly to the moon. Ask for volunteers to come to the front of the classroom and tell the class 'What I want most in the whole world is ...'. Then the rest of the class must come up with all the reasons they can't have it. As they suggest these reasons, the volunteer could come up with ideas for overcoming the obstacles.
- *A series of problems*: As we saw above, a single problem will

cause conflict, but a series of problems (preferably rising in difficulty and danger as they progress) will cause a higher level of tension. To experiment with this, give your students a scenario (for instance, a group of children who go out on a boat), and ask them to come up with a series of problems for the characters to encounter, of increasing danger and complexity. For instance, in the scenario given, their series of problems might run as follows:

- One of the children feels seasick.
- The map falls overboard and they get lost.
- A storm starts to brew.
- The boat springs a leak.
- They find that there is a hole in the lifeboat.
- The boat starts to sink.
- The storm begins to rage.
- The boat sinks and the children are thrown in the water.
- The sharks arrive!

The importance of dramatic tension

Dramatic tension is closely linked to conflict. Dramatic tension is what keeps the reader (or audience) 'on the edge of their seats'. It is what involves us with a story and its characters, and makes us want to read on to find out what happens. Writers can develop dramatic tension through the use of conflict, as described above. However, tension can also be produced in other ways:

- *Vocabulary*: The type of words used when writing a story can be very effective in creating and developing dramatic tension, especially within certain genres. For instance, in a ghost story words such as 'creak', 'howl', 'terror', 'petrified' would all help to keep the reader feeling tense and nervous.
- *Sentence structure*: The length and structure of sentences can also add to the level of tension created, and it is worthwhile studying examples from the thriller or action genres to see how this works. Writers will often use a series of very short sentences to create a feeling of breathy, nervous tension.
- *Imagery*: Similes, metaphors and other images can be used to great effect when adding tension to a story. The images that a writer employs may hint at danger below the surface, as in

the example below, where the gargoyles have 'faces like demons', clearly suggesting that evil is in the air.

- *Lighting and 'special effects'*: The best stories often have a cinematic feel to them, and when we think about films that are full of tension, there is often much use made of lighting and other special effects. It could be that darkness is used to hide the danger that lurks all around, or that a mist suddenly descends on a group of children as they walk through the forest.

- *Sound effects*: Similarly, when watching scary or tense films, sounds will often be used to add to the tension. In the example below, notice how the sound that Danny hears adds to the frightening atmosphere.

- *Character responses*: The way that a character responds to a situation will also help create tension. The reader senses the fear that the character is feeling; for instance when Danny shivers in the example below, this heightens the feeling that danger is close by.

- *The 'cliffhanger'*: A cliffhanger is often found at the end of chapters in novels, but can also be used in shorter stories. The cliffhanger simply leaves the reader 'hanging' in the air, wondering 'what did happen next?'. Sometimes the question is answered, sometimes the writer jumps to a later point in the story, leaving the reader's question unresolved.

- *Enclosed spaces*: Tension is often at its highest when we are confined or restricted in some way. For instance, if a lift gets stuck between floors there is the opportunity for tension to arise (especially if one of the characters in the lift is claustrophobic, or has some other sort of pressing problem).

- *Story questions*: A story question occurs when the reader notices something within the story that seems to be significant. Within the reader's mind, he or she thinks 'Aha! I spotted something important!', and this increases the sense of involvement for the reader. For instance, the writer might mention in passing an object that later turns out to be a clue to the murderer's identity. In the example below, we hear of 'that case in '92', which is mentioned only in passing, but which is clearly going to be significant in the story.

The following example shows how some of these ideas can work together to create a high level of tension. I have used the supernatural genre, as this naturally lends itself to a feeling of danger and fear.

Danny looked up at the dark stone castle, just visible in the deepening gloom. Gargoyles hung from the battlements, their faces like demons, watching him, laughing at him. A cold wind swept down from the distant mountains and made him shiver. He pulled his coat tighter and tried to stop shaking. They had dared him to do this. To go inside. Inside the Castle of Terror. That was what they had called it. He laughed at them when they said that. 'Don't believe in the supernatural, then Dan?' Johnny asked. Dan laughed again. 'Nah, it's rubbish,' he answered, but with a rising sense of dread. 'Dare yeh to spend the night in there, then,' Johnny challenged him. Well, he could not turn back now. He had no choice. And besides, he didn't believe in the supernatural. It was all a load of rubbish.

Suddenly there was a hideous sound, half scream, half moan. Danny spun around. The sound had come from behind him. From the forest. Out of the blackness. He could make out something moving towards him through the mist. He turned back to the building. What should he do? Go into the Castle of Terror? Stay out here? 'It's just Johnny trying to scare me,' he told himself. But as he turned back to the creature, and saw what it was, a scream escaped from his mouth. It was the last sound he ever made.

'We got us a body here, Jim,' the policeman spoke into his radio. 'Looks like some maniac on the loose. Bad injuries, ain't seen nothing this nasty in a long long time. Not since, you know, that case in '92. You better get the forensics team out here right away.'

Dramatic irony

Finally, a technique called dramatic irony can also be put to very good use when injecting conflict into creative writing. This complicated-sounding term is actually quite simple to understand. Dramatic irony describes a situation in which the reader (or audience, with a play) knows something that one or more of the characters do not. For instance, a novel in which the reader knows that the murderer is hiding in the heroine's bedroom. As the heroine climbs up the stairs to bed, tension is created by the reader's urge to warn her about the danger that lies in wait.

Writing scripts

There are a number of differences between writing a script and writing a story, and it is important for students to understand this before they attempt to write scenes or plays of their own. When they first write a script, many children will use a narrator to describe the events that are taking place. Rather than this being a deliberate choice, it tends to be because they are inexperienced in telling a story through dialogue. Resorting to a narrator means that they can put across the action by *telling* the audience what is happening, rather than *showing* them this through what the characters say and do.

The section in this chapter on dialogue will give you some ideas about writing effective speech, and these apply just as readily to scripts as to stories or novels. When writing scripts, do take the time to talk through with your students about exactly what makes this particular form of writing special. Here are some ideas that you might like to consider, including advice on some of the more common pitfalls that students experience.

- *Audience*: A script is written to be performed, rather than read. Scripts are aimed at a 'live' audience (whether in a theatre, watching a television show or film), rather than a reader sitting with a book. When writing scripts, encourage your students to visualize their scripts being performed, rather than viewing them as static dialogue on the page. Some of the best scripts come out of practical work – improvisations in which the storyline and characters gradually appear, and which are then put down on paper.
- *Characters*: In a script, we learn about the characters through the things that they say and do, and the way that they appear. This means the dialogue must work hard to show us what these people are like. The writer might also include stage

directions to show the director or actors how the lines should be spoken, how the characters should move, and perhaps information about costume to help define character.

- *Plot*: The audience can only access the plot through the words and actions of the characters. Many students find it very hard to put across the plot of a story simply through the people involved, and at this point will resort to an onstage narrator to tell the audience what is going on.

- *Setting*: Stage directions may be used to explain the location of the events. However, when a play is performed, the setting can only be shown to the audience by set design, furniture, costume and any special effects. Again, the temptation is for your students to use a narrator who gives this information to the audience.

- *Special effects*: One of the great things about creating scripts is that it gives your students the chance to be inventive with their use of 'special effects'. Although in reality their play might not be performed, there is no harm in them going to town on the imaginative possibilities, including:
  - Lighting: use of colours, bright or dim lights, spotlights, strobe.
  - Sound: animal sounds, machine sounds, traffic noise.
  - Other effects: smoke machines, bangs, etc.

- *Layout*: Before working on scriptwriting, do take time to show your students the correct layout. This will include information such as:
  - List of characters.
  - Details of setting.
  - Not using speechmarks.
  - How to give stage directions.
  - Use of scenes and acts.

Writing poetry

In my experience, younger children respond well to poetry, and really enjoy writing poems of their own. However, by the time students get into the later years of secondary school some of them have been 'turned off' the whole idea of poetry as a form for writing. For this reason, as well as talking about general approaches to teaching poetry in this section, I have also included some ideas for teachers who are finding poetry really difficult to teach, whether because of poor class behaviour or lack of interest.

First approaches to poetry

When approaching poetry writing, I would recommend that you start off by digging into exactly what does make a poem a poem. This is actually surprisingly hard to ascertain. After all, both poetry and prose might include imagery, words that rhyme, rhythmic language, sensory perceptions, and so on. At its heart, a poem is a piece of condensed language, one that creates a strong image or a series of pictures. Poetry is also essentially about sound and rhythm, about the way that words sound when they are spoken out loud. However, even these descriptions do not fit all poems. Here are some questions that you might like to raise with your class.

- What is the difference between a poem and a song?
- If we listen to a song without music, is it a poem?
- Do all poems have to rhyme?
- What is the difference between a non-rhyming poem and a piece of prose?
- How are poems laid out on the page?
- Do all poems tell a story?
- Do all poems have to 'make sense'?
- What makes a good poem?
- Are poems designed to be read on the page, spoken out loud, or both?

Inspirations for poetry

Finding a powerful and engaging inspiration is often the key to success in motivating your children to create their own poetry. The following ideas should give you some ways into writing poems, both for young, emerging writers and for older, more experienced students.

- *Events*: When something important or moving happens, writing poetry can be a good way of dealing with our responses. Writing poems provides an excellent way to express our feelings, to turn our emotions into words. For this reason, poetry may be effective when dealing with PSHE issues within the classroom.

- *Places*: Because of its generally descriptive nature, poetry offers an effective format for creating a 'sense of place', a 'word–picture' that captures a particular setting. You might ask your students to use their senses to brainstorm the sounds, scents, images, and so on, that they associate with a particular place. You could also use poetry as part of the response after a trip to somewhere inspiring.
- *People*: Poetry offers an excellent form for describing a character in detail. Children today live in a celebrity-obsessed world, so you might ask them to write a poem about their favourite famous person. This subject will certainly act as an excellent motivator. Alternatively, they might write a poem about someone they know well, perhaps their best friend, parent, or even (if you're feeling brave) their teacher.
- *Objects*: Just as an artist looks deeply at an object before and during the act of drawing it, so a poet can study something in detail with words. When using an object for inspiration, you might start the lesson with a brainstorm of all the sensory words associated with it, as well as possible narratives connected to the object.
- *Other poets' work*: When approaching a particular topic in poetry, a good way into the work is to show your class samples of work by other poets on that subject. For instance, when introducing war poetry, we might read poems by Wilfred Owen, Siegfried Sassoon, and so on.

The process of poetry

Writing poetry is as much about the process of writing as it is about the finished product. It can take longer to find inspiration for and to edit a poem effectively than it does to actually write the piece itself. It is tempting for children to write a poem and declare it 'finished' without undergoing the processes that lead to a really powerful piece of work. However, if you can encourage your students to spend time working and reworking their poems, they will not only end up with a better finished product, but they will also be practising some of the most important writing skills. Here are some suggestions about how you might prepare your children before they get down to the actual writing of a poem, and how you can encourage them to work and rework the piece once it is underway.

- *Brainstorming*: The brainstorm is tailor-made for the poetry writer, because it encourages us to pick out single striking images that may prove useful in the writing. For instance, a brainstorm on the word 'black cat' might bring out images to do with how the cat moves, looks and sounds. It might also inspire your students to think of other associations, such as witches, darkness and night.
- *The senses*: Good poetry engages all the reader's senses. When you have found a topic for your children to work with, encourage them to think about how each of their senses might be involved. A good way to do this is to use a senses' worksheet (see 'Using your senses', p.84, in this chapter).
- *Sound*: As well as simply reading the words on the page (whether in the 'finished' poem or in the initial drafts), encourage your children to think about the sounds that their poetry is making and to read their work out loud. This might involve exploring alliterative effects within the piece, or it might be about onomatopoeic words and the impact that they have.
- *Cutting*: Often, the fewer words a poem has, the better and stronger the image it creates. When your children have 'finished' their piece, ask them to go back and see which words can be cut out. They might try cutting the total number of words in half, or simply removing any mundane or uninspiring vocabulary.
- *Structure*: When editing poetry, encourage your children to think about the way that the piece is structured, as well as the words it contains. This might involve dividing a poem up into verses, or laying it out in an interesting way on the page.

Motivating those who 'don't do poetry'
It is a pity that there are some students who just 'don't do' poetry, whether writing it or reading it. After all, 99.9 per cent of

modern-day children love popular music, and what else is a song but poetry put to music? I think this is the connection we are missing – a way of making poetry relevant to their everyday lives, rather than seeing it as something 'literary' and perhaps rather middle class. Here are some thoughts about how you can motivate and engage those who believe that they have no interest in poems.

- *Appealing themes*: When working with poorly motivated students, try to find a theme or topic that is going to appeal. For instance, I once taught a class of GCSE students who were poorly motivated when it came to poetry. There was a high percentage of boys in the class, and I was determined to find some way of engaging their interest. I used a variety of poems on the subject of football, such as 'The Ballad of Hillsborough' by Simon Rae, which caught their attention and proved highly motivating for them.
- *Well-known poems*: Students also engage with poems that they know well, or that they associate with a different medium, such as film. For instance, the poem 'Stop All The Clocks', by W.H. Auden, appeared in the film *Four Weddings and a Funeral*. When using this piece to inspire my students, they seem delighted to find that they already know the poem.
- *Appealing forms*: There is a great deal of what we would traditionally call poetry in modern-day musical forms, particularly in rap and hip-hop. These musical styles rely on the spoken word, with a strong rhythmical feel, and you can use this connection within the classroom as a motivator. You might ask your students to bring in samples of their favourite tunes (although keep an eye out for inappropriate language). I have used the idea of rapping very effectively in the classroom when teaching iambic pentameter. By getting the class to 'rap' out the underlying beat on their desks, they gain a much better understanding of what this term means.
- *Songs as poetry*: Type out the lyrics of some popular songs and present them as 'poetry'. I once used this idea for a language-analysis lesson, in which I began by analysing the 'poems' (lyrics) with the class, and then showed them that these

poems were in fact songs. We explored the tone of the poems as written pieces, and then looked at the way in which the music fitted (or didn't fit) the tone we had identified. This work could be followed up by asking your students to bring in songs of their own choice for inspiration and analysis.

- *Something shocking*: I will leave it up to you regarding how far you are willing to go in employing 'shock tactics' (it depends a great deal on your school and the particular age of children that you teach). However, suffice it to say that there are plenty of 'shocking' poems out there (both in terms of subject and language) that might well motivate students who are bored by conventional poetry.
- *Pure analysis*: Sometimes, the least well-motivated children are engaged by the feeling that they are learning something highly technical and analytical. If this is the case with your class, introduce them to the delights of extended metaphors, pathetic fallacy, assonance, alliteration, and so on. You may well find that they surprise you in their level of interest.

6 Non-fiction writing

This chapter introduces you to a range of strategies and ideas for working on the techniques of non-fiction writing. I use the term 'non-fiction' to refer to the form of the writing (instruction booklets, newspapers, and so on) as opposed to the content of or inspiration for the writing. In many of the examples here, I use a creative basis for the content, but ask the students to write *as though* this imaginary content is factual. Of course, non-fiction writing crops up in practically every area of the curriculum. I do hope that teachers from whatever subject background will find some new ideas from this chapter to try out in their classrooms.

Taking notes

For much non-fiction writing, our students need to do research and take notes before they can start work. Learning to pick out key points and take notes from a teacher giving information orally also plays an important role in learning. The key skills in taking notes are to identify the most important or relevant pieces of information, and then find a way of writing these down so that they are easily accessed at a later stage. Below are some ideas about how you might develop these skills with your classes.

- *Practise scanning texts*: Learning to skim or speed read texts is a very useful skill to develop. One useful exercise is to give your students a very limited time to read through a piece of text, time they must use to pick out only the most important words. This approach forces them to utilize their visual reading ability, rather than spending time sounding out each individual word. Your children may surprise themselves at how straightforward this scanning is to do, and with practice it becomes ever easier.

- *Practise annotating texts*: Annotation is closely related to note-taking, because when we annotate we are identifying important words or phrases, underlining or highlighting them, and showing why they are important. The skill of annotation can be taught from an early age, using the very simplest texts, then revisited again and again over the years.
- *Work with listening as well as reading*: As well as taking notes from written texts, train your students to take notes from an oral source. For instance, you might read a story to your class and ask them to make short notes about the important events and characters.
- *Work with an overhead projector*: Seeing the teacher annotating or making notes on an overhead projector or electronic whiteboard will help the students learn this skill. Seeing their teacher as a 'writer' also plays an important part in motivating our children.
- *Use a concise and relevant layout*: Teach your children about how notes can be written in a way that makes them easy to access in the future. For instance, they might use a series of brainstorms to note facts on each topic area.
- *Use colours*: As well as using a layout such as the brainstorm, your students might also use different colours for different subject areas within their notes.

Building your writing

For many students, the temptation is to view writing in the same way that they experience reading – to start at the beginning of a text and to move forwards until they get to the end. However, there is a huge difference between reading a finished piece of text and creating your own writing. The writer of the text being read will normally have spent substantial amounts of time following the steps described in Chapter 3, and this is ideally what you want to encourage your students to do too.

A large part of the process of 'writing' my books actually involves 'building' them. I start with an outline of what the book might include, and only gradually is this outline filled in and the book completed. This approach to writing is especially helpful for your students when they are using computers for written work, which makes the process of editing much simpler.

To give a metaphorical example, building your writing is much the same as building a house. You start with the 'big picture', the overall design of the piece, and then gradually construct the frame and begin to add the walls. It is only when the building is complete that the 'finishing touches' can be added. In the same way, I might first approach a piece of writing with an initial idea or overall plan, then move on to add chapter headings, section headings, and so on. At this stage the writing itself might start, with time spent elaborating each section in turn, and perhaps reordering or restructuring the overall shape of the piece. Finally, I would look through the completed text of a book to 'tidy up' and make the smaller linguistic changes and corrections that finish off the work.

Here is a more detailed explanation of how you might get your students to 'build' their writing, using some of the processes described in Chapter 3. An interesting way to approach this activity with your students could be to use the metaphor described above of building a house.

Building a house	Building a piece of writing
Select the type of house and its location	Select a form for the writing
Know who you are building it for	Know your audience
Think about the style of the house	Think about the style of your writing
Come up with initial ideas	Brainstorm your ideas
Find out technical details	Research facts/information
Make an initial design	Map your ideas/points
Decide on building materials	Select your material
Make a detailed design	Plan your writing
Build the foundations	Build your initial outline
Put up the main structure	Add in details of each section
Build the walls	Start to build the writing

Put on the roof and lay floors	Sort out the introduction/conclusion
Work on the interiors	Edit and rework the writing and structure
Finalize the decorations	Sort out technical and stylistic touches

Non-fiction forms

When writing factual pieces, for instance in history, geography, science, and so on, it can be very useful to be inventive with the forms that you use, especially if you need to motivate your students. For instance, on occasions you might use the newspaper form to write about a historical event, or the recipe form to write out a chemistry experiment. Here is a list of some different forms that have the potential to be used in non-fiction writing across the curriculum:

- Summaries
- Newspaper stories
- Reviews
- Reports
- Detailed analysis
- Essays
- Brochures and pamphlets
- Programmes
- Manuals
- Instruction booklets
- Recipes
- Shopping lists
- Letters
- Emails
- Web pages
- Diaries
- News reports
- Police reports
- Witness statements
- TV programmes

- Magazines, including:
  - articles
  - problem pages
  - letters pages
  - advertisements.

Frames and structures

The Literacy Strategy encourages us to offer our students 'frames' for their work, and this is an excellent idea, especially for the less able, as it helps them structure their writing. When working with these frames or structures, try to get your children to identify the features for themselves, rather than always providing them with a ready-made framework. This will create a sense of ownership of the ideas, and will also help you develop their analytical skills. For instance, you might look at a series of letters with your students, identifying the aspects and features that appear in each one, and then applying these to the children's own work. Similarly, you might read a number of recipes with your class and explore the way that they are structured, and the elements that must be included. These details could be brainstormed in groups, then annotated on an overhead projector or board for the whole class to use.

Technique and non-fiction writing

Technique is just as important when writing a piece of non-fiction as it is when doing creative writing. The word technique might apply to the accuracy of the work in terms of its spelling, punctuation and grammar, but it equally applies to the technique of structuring a piece of writing, or of drafting and editing the work. There is much information earlier in this book about technique: ideas about the basics in Chapter 2, thoughts on developing writing techniques throughout the process in Chapter 3, strategies for effective essay writing in Chapter 4, and also some more creative approaches in Chapter 5.

Two of the key techniques that can be developed in non-fiction writing are described below. The effective use of rhythm and tone will make the difference between a piece of non-fiction writing that is only average, and one that is good or even outstanding.

Rhythm in non-fiction writing

Although rhythm is something we traditionally associate with poetry, all good writing has an internal rhythm of its own. Effective use of rhythm will create a piece of writing that seems to flow naturally, and which sounds right to the reader. The rhythm of writing is made up of a range of components: the sound and length of the words that are used; the way the sentences and paragraphs are structured; the type of connecting words that are used, and so on. Here are some thoughts about how you can help your students develop their use of rhythm.

- *'Hearing' the writing*: In order to explore the rhythm of our writing, we first need to be able to hear it. Ask your children to read their work out loud, to the class or to a partner, or perhaps by making a tape recording. It is also important to develop the internal voice that speaks to us as we write. This is crucial because, when they are writing in exams, your students will not be able to hear their writing out loud.
- *Developing grammatical structures*: If you are working with emerging writers, those who are just learning to put their words down on the page, you may well notice how 'stilted' their writing sounds. Because they have a limited vocabulary and understanding of technique, they tend to use sentences with a basic single clause structure of subject–verb–object. For instance, 'The girl / threw / the ball.' It is only as they develop an understanding of more complex grammatical structures that the writing can start to really flow.
- *Use of punctuation*: The way that a writer punctuates her work will have a strong impact on its rhythm. For instance, if a long sentence is broken up with commas, perhaps a large number of commas, this slows the reader down, forcing him to take breaths, as the sentence you have just read demonstrates. Similarly, the use of questions and exclamation marks will also affect the rhythm of a piece of writing.
- *Vocabulary*: Some words create a strong emphasis within a sentence, forcing the reader to pause for a moment. They

might be longer words, with several syllables. They could also be emotive ones, words that conjure up particular images for the reader. For instance, if I put the word 'horrific' in this sentence, you will probably pause slightly as you read it.

- *Presentational devices*: The use of italics or bold can have an impact on the rhythm and stresses within a piece of writing. If the reader sees the word *horrific*, he will stress it even more strongly because it appears in italics.

- *Mixing sentence lengths*: A piece of writing with a good rhythm will generally have mixed sentence lengths. Short sentences might be used to develop tension or pace, or to give the piece a feeling of simplicity and clarity. Some writers will use a long sentence when a couple of shorter ones would in fact work better. Encourage your children to experiment by breaking down longer sentences into shorter, pithier ones.

- *'Notate' the writing*: When we are analysing the rhythm or metre of poetry, we break down each line into syllables and stresses. We can also do this with narrative or non-fiction writing, for instance counting the number of words and syllables in each sentence, to identify the rhythm that we are using. These could even be written out like a musical score, to explore the overall pattern.

Tone in non-fiction writing

The tone of a piece of non-fiction writing depends a great deal on the reason behind the writing, and the audience that is being addressed. Even if you view your subject area as completely factual, your students will still need to consider the tone in which they write in order to best appeal to their readers. Being able to write with an effective tone is closely connected to finding a voice for our writing. For instance, when writing to complain about something, we might sound indignant or shocked. When writing to instruct we may use a calm, unemotional tone of voice. There are various ways in which we can add tone into our writing, and many of the factors that influence rhythm will also have an effect on tone.

- *The use of questions*: A question, especially within a piece of non-fiction writing, creates a very particular tone. The question might be rhetorical, or it could be a direct question to the reader/audience. It might be asked with a horrified tone, or as a simple query. Using questions tends to slow down or pause the reader, as he considers what his own answer would be. Using questions also creates a strong connection between writer and reader, as the writer is, in effect, directly addressing his audience.

- *The use of statements*: Making statements should always be done with care in non-fiction writing, especially if the subject being discussed is a controversial one, or is not generally considered as 'fact'. The overuse of statements can create quite a pompous tone, as though the writer believes that what he or she says is always right and definitive. Encourage your students to experiment with making interpretations rather than statements. This will help them both in creating tone in their writing, and also in those awkward examination moments when they are unsure if that 'fact' is 100 per cent correct.

- *Use of italic/bold*: As we saw above, putting a word or phrase in italics or bold will have an impact on rhythm, as it creates a strong and emphatic tone. However, these presentational devices should be used sparingly, rather than being scattered throughout the writing. In fact, writers with a strong sense of 'voice' may be able to suggest emphasis simply through the words and structures they use.

The importance of being an expert

The 'role of the expert' is a drama technique that can be used to great effect when working on non-fiction writing. By creating the fiction that your students are a group of experts on a particular subject, and giving them the power that goes along with this role, you will find amazing levels of motivation can be achieved. The students love being taken 'out of' the school setting and put into a fictional scenario in which they have power and influence.

When using the role of experts for non-fiction writing, I have found that one of the best approaches is to use a group project.

This allows the members of the group to utilize their own particular abilities and talents, and also to learn from the people they are working with. I have used this type of 'experts project' very successfully when working with targeted, lower-ability groups, as well as with more able students. You can find some advice below about how to use the 'role of the expert' in your own classroom.

Running a group project

Before setting up and running a group project like this, there are various technical and organizational issues that you should address. The points below are gathered from my experience of actually using these projects within my classroom.

- *Group numbers*: The best number for a group project is about four students. Much more than this, and the groups will find it hard to work together and to stay organized. Less than this, and you will miss out on the different areas of skill that each student brings to the work. Some of your students might want to work in pairs, and you will need to decide whether you are going to allow this.
- *Group mixes*: Group projects offer an excellent opportunity for mixed-ability work. The more able might help out their less able counterparts. The quieter students could keep the over-confident 'leaders' in check.
- *Choice of groups*: Students do tend to work best if they choose their own groups, working with people that they like. If you allow your children to choose the make-up of their groups, ensure that the less popular or quieter children are not left out.
- *Time-scale*: It is important to set a time-scale before beginning this type of work. Otherwise, the project tends to expand to fit the amount of time you are willing to give it. Setting a realistic time-scale and giving your class targets for each lesson's work will help keep them on track.
- *Setting the focus*: To keep your children on task, it is a good idea to write out a worksheet with a series of activities you want them to complete. The group can then divide these activities up so that each person has a specific task on which to focus.

- *Keeping the focus*: It often happens that the students lose their focus, spending excessive amounts of time on an area of the project that they particularly enjoy. To avoid this problem, you could ask your children to agree specific activities that they will complete during each lesson, and also to set themselves homework tasks.
- *Audience*: For most of the projects suggested below, there will be a specific audience for the work. If you can make the audience as 'real' as possible, for instance selling the magazine to other students within the school, this will help motivate your children to produce their best possible work.
- *Presentation*: Do try and give your students the opportunity to present at least some of their work on the computer. This will help them to produce a 'finished product' of which they can be proud.

Ideas for group projects

Below are some suggestions for 'role of the expert' projects across the curriculum. These ideas could be adapted to use with students right across the primary and secondary age range.

- *The personnel managers' dilemma*: The students work as personnel managers, and they have to decide how to save money for their company. This might be achieved by sacking some staff, or in another, more lateral way (it's up to them how they do it). The groups are given a list of staff, with details about their work backgrounds, experience, qualifications, home life, and so on. They must consult together to choose what to do, writing a report on their findings, and presenting their ideas to the class. I have used this activity in English lessons, but it could also prove useful for business studies, maths or citizenship work.
- *The pop group*: The students work in a group, playing the role of the managers of a pop group. They must work on all the different tasks for their group: from writing song lyrics to making a CD cover, from designing posters for the tour to writing a fanzine for the band.
- *The football team*: For this project the group work as managers of a football team. Again, they must write in a variety of

forms for their team. For instance, they design and label a home and away team kit, make plans for a new stadium, write and produce a match programme, and so on.

- *The magazine*: For many children, much of their day-to-day reading will be of magazines. Both boys and girls seem to enjoy reading magazines, on a wide range of subjects from football, music and fashion to computer games. When setting a group project to make a magazine you can choose from a huge range of different subject areas, depending on the area of the curriculum.

Writing for a range of reasons

It is important to think about the reason behind any piece of non-fiction writing. For poorly motivated students, telling them to write simply because they 'have to' is unlikely to lead to successful work. Giving our children a reason for their writing is a good way of motivating them, and it also sets them very clear targets to follow and aims to achieve. Thinking about *why* we are writing what we are writing forces us to consider the appropriate form, tone, structure, and so on. In the following sections I cover some of the many different reasons why we might write non-fiction.

Writing to instruct and explain

When you are working on writing to instruct and explain, one of the main skills you will be teaching is the art of sequencing. This skill is crucial to good writing, as it helps your children learn about ordering ideas or events within any piece of writing. At the earliest age, the skill of sequencing might help with learning to give a story a beginning, middle and end. At a later stage in their schooling, this skill will help your students to write essays and longer pieces of fiction and non-fiction, ordering their ideas in the most appropriate order.

Here are some ideas about writing to instruct and explain, which give you some original ways of approaching this area.

- *Recipes*: Recipes provide an excellent form for writing on a whole variety of topics. One of the main features of a recipe is a sequence of instructions that must be followed in the correct order. Find ways of using recipes in unusual or imaginative ways. You could ask your children to write a recipe for a spell, based on a reading of the witches' spell in *Macbeth* or on an extract from *Harry Potter*. Ask them to decide on a purpose for their recipe, for instance a love potion or a spell to make their teacher obey them. Get them to choose some really gruesome ingredients to spice things up. Another idea for using the recipe form is for the class to write a recipe for their ideal teacher. This might include two teaspoons of laughter, a pinch of strictness, half a pound of smiles, and so on.

- *Instruction booklets*: Anyone who has ever tried to put together a piece of flat-pack furniture will know that good instructions are not necessarily easy to write! Again, try to find an imaginative topic on which to base your instructions, or an unusual audience for which to write. You might ask your children to write instructions for 'How to make a monster', in response to reading an extract from *Frankenstein*. Or you could write a series of instructions on 'How to make your teacher angry' (if you're daring enough!).

- *Mapping*: When we are giving directions, we need to put the steps in the correct order. We might ask our students to write directions to a real place, but we could also offer them a fictional map, perhaps of a treasure island, and ask them to give directions for how to arrive at the treasure.

Writing to complain

Writing to complain can be great fun, as it allows us to put forward a very strong and personal point of view. It provides our students with a good reason for their writing and, in addition, it can lead to some humorous and engaging pieces of work. Writing to complain offers some wonderful opportunities for experimenting with language and tone. Here are some thoughts, ideas and strategies that you might find useful.

- *What's my tone?*: When writing to complain, we need to find the appropriate tone, one that is suitable for the audience being addressed. We need to put across the way we feel, and also ensure something gets done about our problem. Again, develop the idea of 'voice' with your students – how would what I have written sound if I were saying it out loud to my reader? How would it make them feel – angry, irritated, or willing to help me?

- *A sense of purpose*: When we are writing to complain, we generally want to achieve something, whether it is for the council to fill in the holes in the road, or for a company to refund us for a faulty product. This strong sense of purpose gives a wonderful energy to the writing.
- *Complaining and vocabulary*: Writing to complain offers us the chance to use a wonderful range of words and phrases, many of which we probably wouldn't employ in our day-to-day writing. Thus children can extend their choice of vocabulary, and revel in the sound and effect of the words that they use.
- *Catharsis*: Writing to complain is a great way of getting our anger out over an issue. Writing to complain can be used across the curriculum: in a geography lesson your students might write to the local council to complain about pollution, or in a PE lesson to their local MP to complain about a lack of sports facilities.
- *Working on different styles*: There is also the opportunity for work on style, tone and use of vocabulary. A useful approach is to ask your students to write the 'same' letter of complaint, but in a range of different styles, from the calm to the extremely angry. Alternatively, they might start the letter calmly, but get gradually more enraged as the writing progresses.

Writing and personal communication

Personal communication plays a hugely important role in our lives. It is a role that is constantly expanding, as a huge range of different opportunities for communicating open up to us. In the last few years, there has been an explosion in technology that has resulted in wide access to emails, text messages and the internet. Conventionally, the main form of communication has been the letter, and this is still true today, although we might send an email or text message rather than using 'snail mail'. Traditional, formal letters use a fairly strict format, and English teachers teach the necessary form and vocabulary for these. However, newer forms of communicative writing require a different approach. Looking at our use of language in emails and text messages offers some fascinating insights into the way that language changes and develops to suit its medium.

When they are writing to communicate, your students need to make certain conscious decisions that will influence their work. Here are some questions they might like to ask themselves when writing to communicate.

- What do I want to communicate?
- What form is most appropriate for me to communicate with?
- Who or what is the audience that I am communicating with?
- What will this audience expect from my communication?
- How formal does my communication need to be?
- What style of writing should I use to make my communication effective?
- What response am I hoping to receive?

Writing about writing

One of the best ways in which to develop any skill to its highest level is to watch and learn from the 'masters' at work, whether this involves studying football with a professional coach, or learning about a subject at university from academic professors. With writing, we are lucky in that we are surrounded by text in our daily lives, and we have many opportunities to explore how others write successfully (or not). Possibly one of the best ways of developing and enhancing our own writing is to study that of others, particularly those who write professionally. Within the classroom, this might involve the study of language in various non-fiction forms, as well as the study and analysis of novels and other creative writing. A great tip when studying writing is to 'read as a writer and write as a reader'. What this means is to read with a feeling for how the piece has been written, and to write with a sense of what your reader will appreciate.

Writing about language

Analysing and writing about the way that other writers use language helps our students to develop a greater understanding of their own work. The analysis of both simple and complex texts can teach us a great deal, and this study can begin at a very early age. For instance, with our youngest children we might explore how the instructions for a children's board game are written, while with older students we might look at the ways in which advertisers appeal to their market. This analysis of language use can take place across the curriculum, for instance getting your students to study the way a scientific report is written before writing one of their own.

There are various things to consider when studying and writing about language. Here are some questions you might find useful.

- What type of audience is this piece of writing aimed at?
- What age are the audience?
- What type of people are the audience?
- How does the intended audience affect the way the piece is written?
- What form is the writing in?
- Why has this particular form been used?
- What viewpoint is being used (i.e. first- or third-person)?
- What sort of vocabulary is used?
- How simple or complicated is the vocabulary and sentence structure?
- How long is each word or sentence?
- Is the writing difficult or easy to understand?
- How formal or informal is the writing?
- How is the piece structured – what is in each paragraph and why?
- How does the writing start and finish?
- What point or points is the writer trying to make?
- Is the writer trying to convince us of a particular point of view? Does he succeed?
- What tone does the writer use?
- Is the writer feeling a certain emotion or mood?
- Does the writer use any linguistic devices within the piece?
- How is the piece of writing laid out on the page?

- Are there any special presentational devices used, such as different fonts or text sizes?
- Do you find this piece of writing interesting or engaging? Why? Why not?
- What techniques does the writer use that you might be able to transfer into your own writing?

Writing about literature

In the same way that studying and writing about language use can help us develop our own writing, looking at literature in detail can also be very beneficial for our creative work. The closeness of the connection between the acts of reading and writing means that even our youngest children will be able to make a simple analysis of the way books work. By studying the way that authors write, we can help both the youngest and the oldest students to develop their own writing.

Here are some areas of discussion you might like to use when asking young children of about seven years old to analyse the children's books that their younger siblings might read.

- Language devices, for instance the repetition of certain phrases.
- Type of vocabulary, such as short and simple words.
- The way in which the sentences are structured.
- Use of pictures to help with understanding meaning.
- Topics or genres that will appeal to young readers.
- Colourful layout and large print.

Analysing texts

When you are thinking about texts to use with your students, don't forget to include pieces that are topical or fun as well as more serious literature. There is no reason why we should not analyse and write about a story in a comic book or magazine format. When introducing literary study to my students, I have used extracts from books by Stephen King and Patricia Cornwell. The gruesome nature of these pieces of writing has proved wonderfully gripping for my children.

By 'picking apart' texts that have already been written, we can show our children the complexity of good writing. At the youngest age, you might simply ask your children to underline words that are the same within a text, to explore the effect of repetition. With older students, the annotations could include notes in the margins as well. Working with texts should be an active process, one that helps our students develop their own writing. Show your children that it is okay to pick books apart and to scribble notes on them (obviously in pencil or on a photocopy so you don't ruin a school set of books!). In these ways, we can demystify the world of books and writing, and pull down some of the barriers that stand between the reluctant writer and the text.

7 Writing in all the subjects

This chapter focuses on writing in the different curriculum areas. Each subject of the curriculum has its own particular language: both the technical words that are used within the subject, and also the symbolic 'language' specific to many areas – notes within music, numbers within maths, images within art, and so on. Although each subject might have a language of its very own, many of the skills and approaches used within each curriculum area will feed into the writing our children do. They might be planning, selecting and presenting information, problem solving, decision making – all skills that will be of great use to them in working with the written word.

Because of the difficulties that can be associated with teaching writing in practical areas of the curriculum, I have started this chapter by looking at writing in subjects that involve practical work. I move on to give some general ideas for motivating writers across the curriculum, and finally I look at the (English) National Curriculum subjects in alphabetical order. For each of these subjects I give a brief overview of the potential writing skills that can be developed, a short list of lesson ideas, a detailed outline of one specific lesson, and also some key vocabulary. Please note that I have not included English (or drama), as so much of this book will already be of use for teaching writing in these lessons.

Many of the ideas that I give in this chapter are linked by their use of imaginative approaches. By making writing work really creative and engaging for our children, a fun part of their school day, we should be rewarded with high levels of motivation. Clearly, with so many different subjects to cover, there is a limit to how much detail I can give in each one. If you have a fantastic idea for teaching writing in a specific curriculum area, and you would like to see it included in the next edition of this book, then please send it to me at sue@suecowley.co.uk.

Writing in practical subjects

Some school subjects, such as science, require a mixture of practical and written work. Others involve mainly practical activities, with only a limited role for written tasks, for example PE, art and music. When teaching a practical area of the curriculum, there are various problems that teachers might encounter when asking their students to write.

- *Negative attitudes to the writing*: Some students feel very hard done by when we ask them to write in what they view as a practical, rather than academic, subject. This negative attitude can lead to conflict and bad feelings within the classroom or teaching space. Some children really enjoy practical work – often the least able and the poorly behaved, who find it hard to succeed elsewhere in the curriculum. For these children, when the teacher asks for written work this seems tantamount to ruining their only chance of success.
- *Negative attitudes to the subject*: Other children may have a negative attitude towards the subject itself, viewing it as a poor relation to the 'more important' curriculum areas such as English, maths and science. These subject-related attitudes come about for a range of reasons, particularly the lack of statutory exams in these areas and parental attitudes about which school subjects are most important.
- *Poor-quality writing*: If the children do not view the writing as an integral part of the lesson, the teacher might find the students produce only poor-quality work.
- *Poor behaviour*: Similarly, the negative attitudes of some students might lead them into poor behaviour when they are forced to write.
- *'Writing up' rather than writing*: Sometimes, the teacher will set the written task as 'writing up' what has been done in the practical lesson. Although this writing will form an important part of the work, there should also be room for more interesting approaches to writing activities.

- *Finding a writing place or space*: When teaching in an open space such as a drama studio or a gym, there can be problems finding a suitable place or space to write. Having to move the whole class into a classroom to write at desks can cause problems. It might waste lesson time, cause resentment from the class, and also lead to a lack of focus and poor behaviour.
- *Equipment, materials and resources*: Students who turn up expecting a practical lesson might not bring writing equipment or materials with them. The teacher will need to decide whether the students are going to be given exercise books, or whether they are going to write on loose paper (with the consequent potential for losing work).
- *Storing and accessing the writing*: There are also questions to be asked about how and where the work is going to be stored. If it is kept in an area away from the normal teaching space, this can cause problems of access.

Of course, there are lots of ways in which the teacher can overcome all these problems. Many of the tips given below come as a direct result of my experiences when incorporating writing tasks into a practical subject.

- *Make writing time part of the routine*: If you need to incorporate writing into a practical lesson, then set up writing time as part of the routine right from the word go. Clarify exactly where, when and how writing will take place, both in your own mind and for your students.
- *Set clear expectations*: Make your expectations clear – the standard of work required, the equipment that must be brought, and so on. Explain the percentage of lesson time that will be taken up by writing, and make it clear that practical tasks will only be done if the writing is taken seriously as well.
- *Make writing an integral part of the work*: Steer clear of too many 'writing up' style activities. Instead, make sure the writing goes hand in hand with what you do in the practical lessons, feeding into or out of the work and having a clear sense of purpose.
- *Review the lesson in writing*: A good way of integrating writing into practical work is to use written reviews at the end of the

lesson. Giving your children a clear frame or structure for their reviews will help ensure that they write good quality pieces.

- *Use written homework tasks*: If you have serious problems finding somewhere to write in your practical lessons, then you might set written work as homework instead. Homework tasks might include background research, preparation for the next lesson, and so on.

- *Sort out your materials*: Get your writing materials sorted out from the start of the year, introducing these to the children and sorting out any storage issues. If you do not have access to desks, rather than trooping your whole class halfway across the school, you might get a set of clipboards on which the children can write. If your class are going to write on loose paper, then ensure that each child has a folder in which to keep their work.

Motivation across the curriculum

When we ask our students to write there are some approaches we can take, whatever subject or subjects we teach, that will ensure good levels of motivation. Below are some general tips about keeping motivation high right across the curriculum. Many of these ideas are discussed in greater detail elsewhere in this book.

- *Keep it topical*: use current news, TV, celebrities, fads and crazes.
- *Keep it real*: stay as close to 'real life' as you can to show a clear link between school and the real world.
- *Be authentic*: give your students real life situations and materials to inspire their writing.
- *Use 'games'*: word searches, quizzes and competitions all keep motivation high.
- *Ensure success*: for the very weak writers, give tasks that allow them to succeed, such as 'filling in the blanks'.
- *Use 'frames'*: give an outline structure for more complex pieces of writing.
- *Keep it active*: taking an active part in the lesson keeps your students interested and helps them learn.

- *Make it visually attractive*: ask your children to present their writing in an appealing way, and give them attractive materials with which to work.
- *Use fictional approaches*: get your children playing other characters, by using role plays or the 'role of the expert'.

Art and Design

Clearly, the vast majority of work in art and design will involve the use of different visual mediums. The children will learn to communicate what they see, feel or think through using colour, form, texture, pattern, different materials and processes, rather than via the written word. However, there will still be a place for writing, perhaps to:

- Form an integral part of the design process (see the lesson ideas below).
- Write reviews of their own work, or that of others.
- Brainstorm ideas for their art/design.
- Find starting points, for instance from stories or poems.
- Make notes on the success of different ideas, methods and approaches.

Lesson ideas:
- Writing and illustrating an animal story, using the book *Elmer the Elephant* as a starting point.
- Learning to write calligraphy or hieroglyphics.
- Exploring different fonts (perhaps on a computer) and examining the varying effects and moods these might give.
- Creating sculptures of different letters or words.
- Setting up a whole-class 'art show', then making posters to advertise this and writing a newspaper review in response.
- Designing and then writing postcards in response to works of art from different cultures.

Lesson outline – Packaging:
The children examine different examples of packaging, looking at the visual impact of both images and language. They move on to invent a new chocolate bar, cereal, toy, etc., and then design and

create the packaging that goes with it, including suitable wording. As an extension, they could create posters or television adverts to promote their new product.

Vocabulary list:
artefact, canvas, collage, colour, culture, form, genre, line, materials, paint, paintbrush, pattern, pencil, print, sculpture, shape, sketch, space, style, tactile, techniques, textiles, texture, tone, tools, tradition, visual

Citizenship

There is lots of potential in this new area of the curriculum for developing some really imaginative and interesting written work. The students might be:

- Writing to express a personal opinion.
- Examining other people's experiences and views through writing.
- Making notes from research and use of ICT.
- Exploring the media – writing in different styles to affect the reader's opinion.
- Writing for a real purpose, for example to help with voluntary groups or community activities.

Lesson ideas:
- Writing a leaflet to explain the work done by a local community group, and to encourage new volunteers to join in.
- Writing a letter to the local newspaper to express an opinion on a local issue.
- Setting up an election within the school, and asking the students to write individual manifestos to outline their beliefs and policies.
- Looking at crime and punishment – setting up a whole-class trial for different crimes, writing opening and closing arguments for the defence and prosecution.

Lesson outline – The media – GM Foods:
Examining the controversy surrounding recent developments in genetically modified farming. Study some examples of media responses to the GM issue, identifying how use of language might affect public opinion. Divide the class into groups, giving each group a type of media (broadsheet newspaper, tabloid newspaper, publicly funded radio station, TV advert) and a focus either 'for' or 'against' this issue. Ask the students to write a report or script using this specific viewpoint and trying to persuade their audience to agree with their opinions.

Vocabulary list:
citizen, community, cultural, democracy, diversity, duties, economy, election, environment, ethnic, global, government, identity, institutions, international, justice, legal, local, moral, national, neighbourhood, parliament, political, public, rights, social, society, spiritual, values, vote

Design and Technology (DT)

A variety of different writing forms and styles will be used within design and technology lessons: from the initial, scribbled ideas to the finished design folder with detailed notes, work and drawings. Many of the skills developed in DT lessons tie in closely to those skills required for effective writing. These include:

- Planning and sequencing.
- Writing design briefs.
- Listing what a design will achieve.
- Generating, developing and structuring ideas.
- Explaining clearly what a product will do.
- Having a sense of audience – who will use the product, how it should look.
- Creating realistic working schedules, prioritizing and sticking to deadlines.
- Evaluating how well an idea has worked.
- Identifying criteria to judge the quality of a piece.

Lesson ideas:

- Writing instructions for and then building a monster.
- Writing a list of ten products that could be made using an empty plastic bottle.
- Designing and creating new packaging for a familiar product (for example, Coca-Cola), including the design of new text style and language.
- Creating posters or leaflets to promote safety awareness in DT.
- Taking an existing product, for instance a bird box, and brainstorming new ideas about how it might be designed.
- Writing a catalogue of new products in a specific area, for instance tools and other items for the garden.
- Making a new toy for children, and writing a storybook to accompany it, for instance a toy clock and a book about telling the time.

Lesson outline – Castaway:

Tell the class they are going to be 'castaway' on a desert island. They must chose five essential items to take with them. For each item, they should write a list of potential uses and the reasons why they would want to take this particular thing. Once the class has been 'castaway', give out a series of problems that must be solved, using only these items and any natural materials that they might find. Your problems could include: building and starting a fire; opening a coconut for food; catching fish; building a shelter; surviving a storm; and building a raft to escape.

Vocabulary list:

aesthetics, assembly, characteristics, circuit, components, electronics, environment, equipment, function, graphics, hygiene, industry, innovation, manufacturing, materials, mechanical, mechanism, model, modifications, movement, object, opportunity, planning, practical, product, project, properties, reliability, resistant, safety, sensory, software, sustainability, techniques, technology, textiles, tools

Geography

Geography offers some really wonderful opportunities for interesting and exciting written tasks. Many of the techniques that will be used in geography lessons fall closely in line with the key skills and approaches effective writers must develop. These include:

- Asking and answering questions about people, places and environments.
- Investigation and problem solving.
- Viewing issues from different perspectives and then understanding and resolving these issues.
- Exploring their place in the world – values, rights and responsibilities.
- Making and recording observations.
- Collecting and analysing data and information.
- Developing their own opinions and expressing their views.
- Working with secondary sources, such as stories and other texts.
- Finding, recognizing and explaining patterns.
- Undertaking investigations – gathering views and evidence and coming to conclusions.
- Communicating in a way that is appropriate to the task and audience.

Lesson ideas:
- Working as a 'disaster relief team' – researching, planning for and helping out in an area where there has been a natural disaster.
- Drawing and labelling a map of an island where 'pirate treasure' is hidden.
- Writing a tourist brochure and postcards from a foreign country.
- Working in role as a person who lives in another place or country, then writing diary entries to reflect their perspectives and experiences of life.
- Writing a leaflet entitled 'Welcome to Earth', aimed at aliens from another planet, and explaining what the environment is like.
- Investigating the impact of transport on the local environment, and writing a letter to the local council about ways this could be improved.

Lesson outline – School field sell-off:

The lesson starts with the teacher reading out a letter supposedly from the head teacher. This letter explains that the school is going to sell off the sports field to a local supermarket to raise money. The students must then work in role (as parents, students, staff, governors, local people, the supermarket owners, and so on) by holding a meeting at which this issue is debated. In order to support their views, the students should research the impact on their school and local environment of the proposed development. After the meeting, they can write in a variety of forms in response to the lesson. This might include a letter to the local newspaper, a local TV news report, campaign posters for 'save our sports field', and so on.

Vocabulary list:

abroad, atlas, climate, country, county, east, employment, environment, erosion, estuary, features, fieldwork, global, globe, habitat, hill, human, industry, infrastructure, international, landscape, latitude, local, location, longitude, map, migration, mountain, national, natural, north, people, physical, plan, pollution, poverty, regional, river, rural, scale, settlement, south, sustainable, temperature, tourism, transportation, urban, vegetation, weather, west

History

There is huge potential within history lessons for working with a whole variety of written forms. Some of the key writing skills that will be used include:

- Working with chronological order, sequencing and past/present/future tenses.
- Using a variety of sources of information, including stories and eye witness accounts.
- Asking and answering questions.
- Working with information to recall, prioritize and select.
- Creating structured narratives.
- Developing substantiated explanations and coming to conclusions.

- Working with words and phrases that relate to the passing of time.
- Looking at different interpretations and the reasons behind them.
- Selecting and recording relevant information.

Lesson ideas:

- Working as 'time travellers', to go back to a specific historical event, then researching and writing a report from the perspective of people at the time.
- Writing a children's story set in the past, using words and phrases such as 'a long time ago' and 'in the last century'.
- Using an artefact to inspire and develop in role writing, for instance writing diary entries in response to a ration book from the Second World War.
- Writing a fictional 'school report' on a significant figure from the past.
- Writing timelines for different time periods – last week, last year, the twentieth century, 2000 BC to 2000 AD.
- Exploring the symptoms and effects of the plague, and writing 'doctor's reports' about treatment of the sick.
- Writing a newspaper story about stopping the spread of the plague, in tabloid and broadsheet style.
- Creating an 'agony aunt' column in which problems sent in by historical characters are answered.

Lesson outline – Back in time:

Set up your classroom as a village from a particular historical era (for instance the medieval period). The children could dress as characters from that time, and be given the jobs that people would have done. You might use this work to explore living conditions, and how diseases such as malnutrition and the plague could have taken hold as a consequence. Writing that could arise from this setting might include diary entries, newspaper reports, 'aged' documents, and so on.

Vocabulary list:

agricultural, ancient, artefact, castle, century, chronological, civilization, colonization, cultural, decade, defence, disease,

document, dynasty, emigration, eyewitness, government, immi-
grant, independence, industrial, interpretation, invasion, local,
modern, museum, nation, parliament, past, political, population,
present, propaganda, rebel, rebellion, reign, republic, revolution,
settlement, siege, society, time, trade, traitor, world

Information and Communication Technology (ICT)

A great deal of the work that is done in ICT lessons will involve
the use of the written word. Chapter 12 of this book, which deals
with ICT and writing, includes lots of useful information and
ideas for teachers using ICT in any curriculum area. Some of the
writing skills that will be used and developed in ICT lessons
include:

- Research skills – finding relevant information, retrieving it,
  classifying it and checking it for accuracy.
- Interpreting, selecting and organizing information effec-
  tively.
- Considering audience needs in terms of content, quality and
  presentation.
- Developing and refining ideas and subsequently reviewing
  them.
- Investigating and solving problems.
- Writing instructions and creating sequences.
- Asking 'what if' questions.
- Identifying patterns and relationships.
- Finding the best ways of presenting work, for instance DTP
  and multimedia.

Lesson ideas:

- Creating a Powerpoint presentation for aliens, with the title
  'Welcome to Earth'.
- Writing for publication on the internet (see Appendix 2 for
  some website addresses).
- Creating tickets, posters and programmes for a school play.
- Writing a whole-class 'chain story' using email, with each
  recipient adding one line to the story.

- Planning, designing, writing and editing a class or school magazine, using a DTP program.
- Creating frames, templates or macros for different written forms, for example letters, recipes, newspaper articles.

Lesson outline – Safety on the net:
The students work in groups to develop and make a pamphlet concerning internet safety, aimed at children lower down the school. They must analyse their audience's needs, researching pre-existing attitudes to internet usage. They should research the topic and audience in detail before starting, for instance making notes about any cases in the media, writing in a way that will suit the projected audience, using effective presentation, and so on. When the pamphlets are completed, they could be tested out on the projected audience and notes could be made on the children's responses.

Vocabulary list:
application, communication, computer, database, digital, font, format, graphics, hardware, icon, internet, keyboard, macro, mouse, multimedia, network, program, screen, server, simulation, software, spreadsheet, technology, template, toolbar, video, website, wordprocessing

Maths

The language of maths is that of numbers, shapes, and so on. Most of the work that takes place in maths lessons will involve the use of this mathematical language. There are, however, many skills and techniques within the subject of mathematics that feed into, and from, the writing that our children do. These include:

- Intellectual processes, such as logical organization, structuring and breaking down problems, moving step by step, and sorting and classifying.
- Precision – specifying problems, summarizing, checking for accuracy.
- Use of questions: 'If … then …', 'What if …?'.
- Making inferences and deductions, creating and examining theories.

Lesson ideas:

- Improvising and then writing down 'real life' scenes, for instance buying items in a shop.
- Writing fun and imaginative 'If … then …' questions, for instance 'If each alien from the Planet Zog has three legs and five arms, then how many limbs do twenty Zogian aliens have?'
- Creating maths-related storybooks to teach counting or other skills to young children, and then trying these out on a class lower down the school.
- Designing a board game for young children, in which they must match mathematical symbols and shapes to the correct vocabulary.

Lesson outline – Maths at the match:

This idea can be adapted to use with any topic that your children particularly enjoy. Ask the class to write a series of mathematical questions relating to Bob's journey to the football match. These can vary in difficulty depending on the age and ability of the students. For instance: 'If the football match starts at 3pm, and it takes Bob 1 hour 15 minutes to get there, what time should he leave his house?' For a more able or older class, the question might be: 'If the football match starts at 3pm, and the train journey to the ground takes 45 minutes, what time must Bob leave if he wants to arrive 20 minutes early?'

Vocabulary list:

addition, angle, amount, approximately, average, calculate, centimetre, circle, circumference, classify, cube, data, decimal, diameter, digit, division, equal, equilateral, fraction, graph, hexagon, horizontal, kilogram, measure, metre, minus, multiplication, number, numerical, patterns, prediction, quadrilateral, radius, rectangle, rotation, shape, sort, space, spatial, sphere, square, subtraction, symmetrical, triangle, vertical, volume, weight, zero

Modern Foreign Languages (MFL)

Although the emphasis is increasingly on speaking the target language, there is of course huge potential for developing writing in MFL lessons. Despite the fact that the students are working in another language, many of the skills that are practised during MFL lessons will be of great value for their writing in English and across the curriculum. Some of these skills include:

- Knowledge about language itself – looking into grammar, expression, structures, tenses, types of word.
- Adapting writing to suit its context, purpose and audience.
- Writing for real purposes – sending messages by letter or email.
- Writing in a variety of contexts – social, workplace, and so on.
- Summarizing and reporting, taking notes.
- Writing authentic materials – newspapers, magazines, brochures, and so on.
- Redrafting writing to improve accuracy and presentation.
- Writing signs, labels, instructions.

Lesson ideas:
- Finding and writing emails or letters to a penpal in a country where the target language is spoken (see Appendix 2 for website addresses).
- Creating magazines on specific topics in the target language, for example a pop magazine in French, a sports magazine in German.
- Writing a short language course for young children in the target language, with fun games and activities, and colourful presentation.
- Taking a fictional 'plane journey' (the teacher lines the desks up in rows and pretends to be an air steward) and then making and writing postcards from the country home.
- Reading recipe books and then writing recipes in the target language for delicious dishes.
- Role plays in various situations – the shop, the office – followed by writing the scripts of the scenes.

Lesson outline – David Beckham's Assistants (Spanish):
This lesson uses a topical overseas connection, and the 'role of the expert' (see pp.113–6) to ensure full involvement and motivation

from the children. The students work as personal assistants to David Beckham (or any other famous figure who has recently moved to work overseas). They must help him plan for his move to Madrid by completing a variety of tasks, including finding and listing possible accommodation, creating a booklet of 'key phrases' in Spanish for him to learn, giving details of cultural events, local restaurants, and so on.

Vocabulary list:
(note – the majority of vocabulary used will obviously be in the target language) adjective, adverb, audience, conversation, context, country, culture, dictionary, expression, grammar, intonation, language, linguistic, memorise, native, noun, pronunciation, purpose, speak, speech, tense, verb

Music

Just as with art, music offers a way for our students to express themselves in a language other than that of words. The majority of activities will involve listening to, exploring, and creating music. However, the written word might be used in a variety of ways, including to:

- Brainstorm initial ideas for the focus of a piece of music.
- Create lyrics for songs or chants.
- Write about the music of other cultures, both past and present.
- Reflect on, record, and write reviews of what has been achieved in lessons.

Lesson ideas:
- Explore a range of song lyrics from films, asking the students to write their own lyrics for a new or current movie.
- Bring in an unusual object, such as a coconut, then get the class to brainstorm ideas about how this might be used as an inspiration for a piece of music.
- Look at reviews in a variety of music magazines, using these as a basis for writing a review of a piece of music created in class.

- Create a rhyming dictionary, giving lists of rhymes for words, to use when writing song lyrics.
- Write the lyrics and music for a new and up-to-date school song, perhaps based around the school motto.

Lesson outline – Protest music:
The students work in role as the guests and audience on a chat show, exploring different types and forms of protest music. The guests might include famous singers/musicians, such as Bob Marley, Ms Dynamite, Bob Dylan, etc. Members of the audience could question them about how their music provides a format to put across their beliefs. The class could move on to look at examples of different lyrics and to write their own protest songs.

Vocabulary list:
bass, chant, classical, clef, compose, duration, dynamics, genre, guitar, improvise, instrument, jazz, keyboard, lullaby, melody, performance, piano, pitch, play, rehearse, rhythm, silence, sing, sounds, style, tempo, texture, timbre, tradition, treble, tune, vocal

Personal, Social and Health Education (PSHE)

PSHE offers some wonderful opportunities for writing in a wide range of forms, and for a whole variety of different audiences. Because the subject is very much a study of themselves and their relationship with the world, the children will view the work as being real and relevant to their lives. The writing the students do might be based on a whole range of topics, including:

- Personal likes and dislikes, feelings, opinions and views.
- The setting of personal goals and targets.
- Looking after themselves – health, hygiene, safety.
- Examining their own behaviour, and that of others.
- Topical issues – what is right and wrong.
- How we might improve or harm our environment.
- Real choices about areas such as healthy eating, television and money.

Lesson ideas:

- Designing posters and other materials for a 'Stop the bullies' campaign.
- Running a 'Save the environment' campaign within the school, including posters to encourage recycling, anti-litter notices, researching local recycling initiatives, etc.
- Creating a list of 'my personal goals', giving five targets for self-improvement, either within school or at home.
- Writing a story about where they want to be, and what they want to be doing, in 10, 15 or 20 years' time.
- Planning, writing and illustrating a book for children called 'My body'.
- Writing a webpage on road safety for pedestrians, cyclists and drivers.
- Writing a list of all the things that are good about one of their classmates.
- Scripting a class assembly on a topic such as racism or HIV.
- Creating a problem page, on which they work as agony aunts and uncles to answer common concerns of children their age.

Lesson outline – 'Who wants to be a millionaire?':

You might like to start this activity by watching an extract from the TV programme, in which the contestant wins a large sum of money. Now ask your children to imagine what it would be like to have this much money. Tell them to write a list of 10 or 20 things that they would do or buy with the money. Ask them to think carefully about the impact of their choices. Would they share the money, or spend it all themselves? How might other people feel towards them after their win?

Vocabulary list:

behaviour, bullying, career, citizen, community, contraception, disease, diversity, divorce, drugs, environment, family, friends, global, healthy, hygiene, law, legal, puberty, racism, responsibilities, social

Physical Education (PE)

Clearly, the majority of activities in PE lessons will be physical, practical ones. However, there are some areas of the subject that will benefit from or require the use of the written word. These include:

- Planning and evaluating actions, ideas and performances.
- Remembering sequences, moves or actions.
- Understanding the rules and conventions for different activities.
- Planning, using and adapting strategies; tactics and compositional ideas.
- Study of the physiological aspects of sport.
- Safety issues.

Lesson ideas:

- Writing a survival booklet giving lists of equipment and safety factors for an orienteering activity.
- Creating posters or lists of rules concerning safety within PE generally, or within a specific sport.
- Writing a comic strip to show the correct technique for different moves within a game.

Lesson outline – Instruction booklet:

After learning a new game, such as rounders, basketball or netball, the children write an instruction booklet about the rules and directions for playing the game. To make this activity more engaging, you could ask them to choose an unusual 'audience' for their writing, such as an alien with three arms, telling them to alter the rules to fit this unusual player!

Vocabulary list:

action, activity, apparatus, choreographer, coach, competition, competitive, coordination, dance, direction, equipment, exercise, fielding, gymnastics, hygiene, jump, movement, official, performance, performer, referee, rhythm, rules, sequence, strategies, swim, tactics, team, throw, turn

Religious Education (RE)

There are plenty of opportunities within RE lessons for writing in a variety of forms and for a range of purposes. The use of stories and texts plays an integral role within the subject. Students might be writing to develop their work and ideas in many ways, including:

- Considering questions of meaning and purpose in life.
- Developing knowledge and understanding of different religions.
- Expressing, reflecting on, analysing and evaluating beliefs.
- Developing a sense of identity and belonging.
- Identifying puzzling questions, and finding answers.
- Looking at the beliefs and cultures of others.
- Sharing the celebrations of different faiths.

Lesson ideas:
- Looking at the calligraphy in early religious books, and then writing a poem or story about their own beliefs, using calligraphy to present it.
- Making posters, cards or decorations to celebrate a variety of festivals.
- Considering the role of symbolism, for instance writing about the symbolic nature of light within different faiths.
- Writing newspaper or magazine articles about key figures within different religions.
- Updating stories from sacred texts, rewriting them within a present-day context.
- Making a book of religious stories for young children.

Lesson outline – Newspaper article:
Writing a report on the death of Jesus during a study of early Christianity, as seen in the newspaper *The Jerusalem Echo*. The report could include descriptions of the crucifixion from Roman soldiers, interviews with the followers of Jesus, quotations taken from the Bible, and so on.

Vocabulary list:
baptism, Bible, biblical, Buddhism, Buddhist, celebration, ceremony, Christian, commandment, community, creation, disciple,

ethical, faith, festival, Hindu, Hinduism, hymn, Islam, Islamic, Jewish, Judaism, miracle, morality, Muslim, parable, pilgrimage, prayer, prophet, religion, religious, shrine, Sikh, Sikhism, spiritual, symbol, synagogue, temple, values, worship

Science

Science offers plenty of opportunities for our students to develop key writing skills. Although the work will involve lots of practical approaches, even during these activities the children will be learning techniques that can feed into and out of their writing. These include:

- Using precise language and meaning, taking context into account.
- Asking questions – 'how', 'why', and 'what if'.
- Following instructions.
- Working in a logical and coherent way.
- Exploring – making use of the senses.
- Making comparisons, finding patterns and associations.
- Labelling and creating diagrams.
- Grouping, classifying and sorting by characteristics.
- Working with lots of different vocabulary, for example: changing materials – bend, squash, twist, stretch; circulation – heart, blood, vessels, pump.
- Coming to conclusions, testing explanations.

Lesson ideas:
- Ask the children to 'imagine you are a . . .' (bird, rock, atom, etc.) and to write from this perspective about their experiences and the way they see the world.
- Use nursery rhymes to explore different scientific ideas, for instance *The 3 Little Pigs* to examine building materials. From this they could write instructions to make a stable building, diaries of a pig's day, and so on.
- Get the class to write a hypothesis based on 'What would happen if . . .?'. Some ideas could be: 'What would happen if wheels were square?' or 'What would happen if there were no clouds?'

- Blindfold some volunteers and give them various objects or substances to touch, smell or taste. Ask the class to write about their sensory responses to these different things.

Lesson outline – Journey into space:
The teacher puts the chairs in the classroom into rows, in the same layout as on an aeroplane. The children are told that they will be going on a journey into outer space, in their very own spaceship. As they fly away from the Earth, you could introduce the various planets that they travel past. They could be asked to make a 'logbook' for the spaceship, writing down notes about each planet they pass. Another written response to this might be for them to send letters home to their families, describing the different planets they have seen. To make this work more exciting, your spaceship could encounter some asteroid belts on the way, which hit the spaceship and throw the children about inside!

Vocabulary list:
absorb, acid, alkaline, apparatus, biological, cell, chemical, circuit, circulation, condensation, conductor, digestion, dissolve, distil, element, enzyme, evaporation, experiment, forces, friction, function, gravity, growth, habitat, hazard, insulator, laboratory, liquid, magnetic, mammal, materials, measure, minerals, nitrogen, nutrient, observations, organism, oxygen, particles, permeability, physical, plants, prediction, properties, reproduce, respiration, sample, scientific, senses, skeleton, soluble, solution, temperature, test, thermometer, vertebrate, vessel, vibration

Part 3

Writing it Right

8 Writing and assessment

Most of the writing that our children do in school will of course be assessed in some way, whether it is marking their exercise books, keeping a record of work to assess their progress in class, or writing for externally assessed examinations. However, we should never consider that our students are writing *for* assessment – the writing will (or should) always have a reason, and an audience, beyond this. This chapter deals with the assessment of writing. I give some thoughts and ideas about how teachers might approach assessment and mark their students' writing in the most effective way. I also look at how we can help our students deal with their writing and its assessment in public examinations.

Increasingly, it seems, we are being asked to assess and grade our children's work from a very early age. While this is not the place for a discussion of the rights and wrongs of this approach, I do feel strongly that such constant testing can erode the self-esteem of those who most need help – those for whom writing is a real struggle, and those whose motivation is low. As we mark and assess our students' work, we do need to be aware of the potential damage that can be done to our poorly motivated children, those with special needs and the least able.

Marking writing

When we mark a piece of writing, we are effectively making a judgement, acting as both reader and reviewer of what the child has produced. This is a very powerful position to be in. Making judgements on someone else's writing needs to be done with care and sensitivity, because writing is such a personal thing, such a reflection of our own personality. Our ultimate aim should be for the children to play both roles – to be able to read, review (and consequently edit) their own work, until they are happy with the end result and ready to show it to an audience if they wish.

When we do mark our students' writing, we need to think carefully about the purpose of the assessment, about what we are actually marking *for*. In some subjects, and for some teachers, the content of the writing may be far more important than the student's expression or use of technique. For other teachers (and increasingly for all teachers, with the National Literacy Strategy coming into play), judgements have to be made about technique as well as content, with the teacher considering how well the child has actually written, in addition to assessing the content of the work.

It is fair to say that at times, when we are overburdened with paperwork or any of the myriad pressures of our jobs, marking becomes little more than a paper exercise – a job that needs to be done, but with little thought about the reasons behind it and its potential benefits. If we are honest, this type of marking is pretty much worthless in educational terms. It is at times like these that we need to return to our original motivation for marking, which is primarily to help our students learn, to help them understand what is good and bad about their written work, and how they might improve it. Here are just some of the different ways in which marking can help in this learning process.

- Showing a child where he has made errors.
- Helping him to learn why he has made these mistakes.
- Helping him to avoid making the same mistakes again.
- Showing him what is good or effective about his work.
- Helping him learn why these particular aspects of his writing are effective.
- Helping him to repeat the effective parts of what he has written.
- Making the child feel positive about his written work, to help motivate him.
- Praising the child for what has gone well, to encourage him in the future.

Marking symbols
Marking the technical aspects of a piece of writing can take a

surprisingly long time, especially if you write out corrections in full. This is where marking symbols come in handy, helping to make the job of marking much faster and more efficient. Sharing these symbols with our students should also enable them to correct their own drafts more quickly and effectively.

You can find some of the more commonly used symbols in the resources section at the back of this book (see Appendix 4). An excellent way of encouraging your students to use and understand these symbols is to photocopy them to go in the front of student exercise books, and going through their meanings with your class. Even the youngest children should be able to understand and use at least some of these symbols.

Different ways of marking

Marking comes in many forms: from the helpful to the destructive, from the specific to the generalized. Detailed marking can be incredibly time-consuming, and it is vital for the teacher to make some decisions about what will be marked, and in how much detail. It's a balancing act – we just cannot, as working teachers, mark every single piece of work in full detail. Below are some thoughts on the different systems of marking that you might use, and some comments on the advantages and disadvantages of each method.

- *Close marking*: Many people (including parents, managers and inspectors) view this as the ideal form of marking. With this style of marking, each and every error is identified, and detailed comments are made on how the student can improve her work. Close marking does have its drawbacks: it is very time-consuming for the teacher, and it can be offputting (and sometimes damaging) for students to receive back their writing completely covered in the teacher's pen. However, close marking can be very successful in helping older and very able students to develop complex pieces of writing such as essays.
- *Tick and flick*: This type of marking involves placing a big tick (or cross) at the end of each question, paragraph or page, then turning (or 'flicking') to the next. A brief comment may be made at the end of the piece of writing. Although we

might be able to say that we have 'marked' the children's work, this method is not particularly effective when it comes to the students actually learning from their mistakes. However, children do like their work to be 'marked'. In addition, the teacher can gain a sense of how well the children are doing and which areas need further work.

- *Marking for specific errors or features*: With this type of marking, the teacher identifies an area of concern, or a feature on which he would like the students to concentrate before the writing takes place. For instance, the children might be asked to focus particularly on getting their punctuation right, or to think carefully about how they paragraph their work. The teacher then looks closely at these specific aspects as he marks the work.

Of course, the majority of us employ marking strategies that fall somewhere in the middle of all the above, depending on the amount of time we can afford to give to marking the work. It is useful sometimes to step back and consider how the marking that you do actually impacts on the quality of your children's learning. Although 'ticking and flicking' might make their books 'look' marked, how much good is this form of marking actually doing? If you tend to focus more on 'close' marking, consider whether your students might feel that this implies a criticism of their writing, and whether it might be demotivating for them.

Strategies for marking

Because of the time-consuming nature of marking, it is useful to consider strategies for making the job more effective and less time-intensive. It is tempting to view marking as something that the teacher does for the children, but this need not always be the case. In fact, some of the best learning can come from employing more unusual approaches. Here are some ideas for you to try, which will also save some of your valuable time. (These approaches would obviously need to be used in conjunction with the teacher's marking.)

- *Marking each other's work*: Asking your children to swap over their writing, and to make evaluative comments on their classmates' work, can be a very effective marking strategy.

The children really enjoy the chance to 'play teacher'. This strategy can help motivate your students, as it shows them what others within their peer group are achieving. Looking at other people's work (whether 'good' or 'bad') will also help them consider what constitutes effective writing.

- *Marking the work together:* There are many opportunities for written work to be marked as a whole-class activity, especially where there are definitive right answers, for instance with spelling tests. The teacher gives the answers while the students tick or cross each one and put a mark or grade at the end. The students could mark their own work (if you trust them!) or they could swap over and mark somebody else's.

- *Marking across peer groups:* An interesting alternative, especially for the secondary teacher with several teaching groups, is to ask your older students to mark the work of their younger counterparts, and vice versa. This is particularly useful where you have a class underachieving (for instance, in Year 9) and another group with high levels of achievement (for example, in Year 7). The embarrassment of marking work that is actually better than theirs, although done by younger students, should make them buck up their ideas.

Approaching exams

As exam time approaches, students can start to experience high levels of stress. This time will probably be especially difficult for your weakest students, who may be used to 'failing'. It could also be that some of your more able students do not perform to the best of their ability when under the pressure of time. There are various ways in which we as teachers can help our students approach exams.

- *Give them plenty of practice:* The more exam practice students have, the more comfortable they will feel with the idea of the approaching exam.
- *Teach them how to revise:* Spend time teaching your students useful revision strategies. You might show them techniques for memorizing facts, or demonstrate the use of brainstorms for creating revision notes.

- *Boost their self-esteem*: Make it clear to your weakest or most nervous students that exams are not the 'be all and end all' in life. Although SATs, GCSEs and A Levels are clearly important for their future, you as a teacher will still value them as individuals, whatever grades they achieve in their exams.
- *Take advantage of their increased motivation*: As exam time approaches, students generally become much more motivated. They realize that it is important for them to do well, and will tend to work harder in class. Take advantage of this increase in motivation, perhaps by focusing on important coursework, or by getting them to write high-quality pieces for teacher assessment.

Preparing for exams

There is no magic 'secret' to doing well in exams – there's simply a range of strategies and approaches that can be learned. Prepare your students for their written exams by giving them information about what the exam will involve and also by showing them how to get the best possible results for their level of ability. For some children with special needs, additional help or time may be allowed in the exams. Check with your examinations officer in advance if this applies to any of your students. Here are some ideas about how you might prepare your students for their exams.

- *Practice, practice, practice*: If you teach an 'examination year', exam practice should become a regular part of your classroom routine. There are a number of good reasons for this.
  - With regular practice your students will realize that there is little to be scared of in exams.
  - They will get used to the general format of the exam paper and start to understand what the examiners want them to do.
  - They will learn about timing – how to allocate the correct amount of time to each piece of writing.
  - They can be educated in the way that exams run – the importance of working in complete silence, and not glancing across at what their friends are doing.

- Although exam practice can add to your marking load, you will get a number of 'lessons off' from teacher-led work.

- *Plan, plan, plan*: There is no need to always write out a full exam answer when you are doing exam practice. A good-quality plan will show you whether or not the student understands how to answer the question. Planning in class also helps your students understand the importance of this part of the writing process, and to practise the skills involved.

- *Information is power (1)*: Get your hands on some old exam papers to share with your students. There is nothing more frightening than the unknown – facing an exam paper never having seen a similar one before will be confusing for your children. They may waste time trying to understand what the exam paper is asking them to do, time that would be better spent proving their abilities.

- *Information is power (2)*: Show your students the marking criteria as well. To gain maximum marks, they need to fulfil these criteria. It is therefore essential that your students understand what they must aim to achieve. For instance, how vital is good technique – accurate spelling, punctuation, etc.? What level of technical language or understanding do they need to demonstrate?

- *Show them sample essays*: A good way of demonstrating how to earn the best possible mark is to show your students a sample essay or exam answer. This might be from a high-quality candidate in a previous year's exam, or it could be an essay that you write yourself to show how the question is best answered. You might also ask the students to give a mark for this answer, using the marking criteria.

- *Work on sample answers as a whole class*: A good way of approaching exam practice is to split your class into groups, and ask each group to formulate an answer, sharing their ideas with the class. This takes away the pressure of individual work, and allows all the students to contribute their own ideas.

- *Show the connection between questions and marks*: Some students fail to understand that a set amount of marks are available for each exam question. Explain to your children that:

- There is no point in writing copious amounts for a question that will only ever earn them two or three marks.
- Some questions are worth answering in detail, because they offer the chance to earn a high number of marks.
- If a question has a number of marks available, the students will often be given one mark for each separate point they make on the subject.

- *Show the importance of timing*: Exam success has much to do with the ability to time your writing. Self-discipline is required to avoid using up the time available without answering all the questions. Practice under exam conditions will help your students learn about timing. If the exam involves writing long essays, tell your students to write the time that they should finish each essay on the answer booklet. If they run over this time, advise them to start the next essay while leaving space to finish the first one, if they have spare time at the end of the exam.

- *Show the importance of the question's phrasing*: Exam questions tend to be phrased in a way that encourages the student to give the correct answer, in the correct form, and referring to the appropriate material. As you spend time going through old papers, take time to look at the language of the questions. Here are some useful discussion points to guide your students:
  - Is the question in two or more parts?
  - Do the different parts earn you equal marks, or is one part more important than another? (Some exam questions look like they only have one part, for instance when they are written in a single paragraph, but are actually asking two separate questions.)
  - Does the question say something like 'According to the passage what does . . .'? If it does, the students must make close reference to the passage in their answer, or use relevant quotations.
  - Does the question ask you to use a specific form or layout in your answer?
  - What tone should be used for this form?
  - Is there a particular viewpoint that is best for answering this question?

  – How much detail do you need to give to receive the maximum amount of marks?

Answering exam questions

As well as preparing your students for their exams, you can also help them with writing their answers. For many, these strategies are not immediately obvious, and they do need to be taught what they are, and how to use them. Here are some ideas you might like to share with your class.

- *Choosing the question*: If the paper gives a choice of questions, talk with your students about how they might choose the best one to answer. This might involve knowing about their individual strengths or being clear about what you have studied in class.

- *Sticking to the question*: You can find lots of ideas about this in Chapter 4 ('Answering the question', pp.67–8). Reassure your children that there is no need to write down everything they know on a subject. If the material they include does not answer the question, they will earn no marks for it.

- *Use the question to start your answer*: Many children find it really hard to get started in exams. Using the wording of the question to begin an answer helps overcome this, and keeps the student 'on track'.

- *Keep it simple*: Your more able children might start to over-complicate things in exams, assuming that the answers must be more difficult than they appear to be. Encourage your students to take a step back from the paper, consider carefully what is being asked, and then word their answer simply and clearly.

- *Don't waffle*: Similarly, some children feel the need to write at great length, when a brief answer would in fact be better. This can cause problems with timing, and it might lose them marks if the examiner feels they haven't stuck to the question. Encourage students with a tendency to waffle to look closely at the marks available for each answer and write only what is needed to earn those marks.

9 The writing clinic

This chapter provides a 'writing clinic', in which some of the most common writing problems are explored, using a series of case-studies. For each case-study, I provide an example of the problem, a 'diagnosis' of why the specific problem is occurring, and strategies for the teacher to use in overcoming the child's particular area of weakness. I have included writing from a range of different ages, to illustrate the problems at different stages in a child's school career.

Over writing

> The ripe orange sun bled into the dark blue sea, like a huge orange being squeezed of its juice. A soft, gentle breeze caressed the pure white sand of the beach. The pretty young girl swept her long curling blonde hair back from her face and sighed deeply, a sad, mournful look on her pale, smooth skinned face.
>
> 'Oh John. How beautiful it is here. What a wonderful day I've had with you. I'm so sad that it has to end.'

Diagnosis

This piece of writing has everything but the kitchen sink! It is melodramatic rather than realistic, and it sounds like something from a romance novel. The writer loves using description and descriptive words, particularly adjectives, and the way that she can make them sound. She may have recently learned about similes and other language devices, and be trying to experiment with them (although not very successfully). She enjoys writing, but has little sense of how her writing might appear to the reader.

Strategies

- *Get an overview*: Ask the student to step back from the work and look at its overall effect. Reading it out loud, perhaps to another student, might help.
- *Write as a reader*: Encourage the student to 'write as a reader' – viewing her work as it would be seen by someone reading it.
- *Find a tone*: Ask the student to read the piece in a variety of different tones, from the 'plain' to the 'pacy' to the 'melodramatic', to see which one fits best to what she has written. This should give a sense of how overwritten the work actually is.
- *Experiment with different tones*: Now ask the student to rewrite the piece, using a completely different tone and style. For instance, rework it as a children's story.
- *Talk about adjectives*: Identify what an adjective is, if the student does not already know. Now ask her to rewrite the piece, removing all the adjectives, and finding other ways to put across any description that is required.

Dull or under-writing

The boy went into the room. There was a table and four chairs in the room. He went over to the chairs and sat down. While he waited for the man to arrive he looked around the room. Then he looked at his watch and wondered when the man would come.

Diagnosis

This writing is 'under written' because of the total lack of description. There is a very limited use of vocabulary. The piece is also dull, because nothing of any real interest happens.

Strategies

- *Consider the choice of verbs*: Ask the student to look at the verbs he has chosen and to try and find more interesting alternatives that suggests something about the boy's character, mood or emotions. For instance, instead of the verb 'went', the boy might have 'strode' or 'stormed' into the room.

- *Consider the use of descriptive language*: Although it's important to avoid an overly descriptive, adjective-laden style, the reader needs some type of detail to be able to visualize what is happening. For instance, when the boy looks around the room, what does he see?
- *Write a detailed study*: Get the student to write a detailed study of one thing inside the room, for instance describing the table in detail. Focus the writing by asking questions, for instance:
  - What material is the table made of?
  - Is it new or old?
  - What size and shape is the table?
- *Consider the development of character*: To give a stronger sense of character, the student could add some more interesting verbs, and write more detailed description. Ask the student to empathize with the character − what is he thinking and feeling and how might this be shown in the way that he moves or reacts to his situation?
- *Add some conflict*: Find ways to encourage the student to add conflict to the piece. Look at the advice in Chapter 5 (pp.94−6) for some tips about how to do this.

Stilted writing

Jane was five. It was her birthday. For her birthday she got a toy. The toy was nice. It was a doll. She played with the doll. She had a party. She had fun.

Diagnosis
This writing is typical of the early, or emerging, writer. It has a stilted style and does not yet flow sufficiently well, making the reader feel that it is very disjointed and 'choppy'. The student does not yet have a sufficiently wide vocabulary to avoid the standard single-clause 'subject−verb−object'-type sentences. The student needs to find some way of joining up the sentences.

Strategies

- *Use of connectives*: The writer needs to develop her 'bank' of connecting words, so that the short sentences can be joined together. The teacher could provide a list of connecting words to try out on this piece of writing, for instance 'and', 'but', 'then', etc.

- *Use of description*: As in the example above of 'dull' writing, the child is not giving the reader any sense of what the people and objects are like. One way of helping might be to ask for a detailed description of the doll, using some questions as a prompt:
  - What does she look like?
  - What colour are her clothes?
  - What is her hair like?
  - What expression is on her face?

- *Developing character*: Again, the writer needs to think about her character, and the way that she is feeling. So far, we only know that Jane had 'fun'. Talk to the child about how her character felt at the birthday party. What did she eat? Did she have a cake, what did it taste like and did she enjoy it?

Lack of punctuation

Sammy raced out of the door and ran down the street he was late for school and he knew that he would get into trouble when he got to school. when he got to school he sped into the classroom but the teacher had already taken the register and Sammy got into trouble again he hated getting into trouble. why are you late again Sammy the teacher asked I woke up late Sammy said because my alarm didnt go off then you need to mend your alarm the teacher told Sammy. youre in detention with me after school now get on with your work

Diagnosis

This child's writing has a strong sense of pace, but is almost completely lacking in punctuation. In a rush to get the ideas own, he has become wrapped up in telling the story rather than thinking about the needs of the reader.

Strategies

- *Reading back*: Ask the student to read his work back to you. This will help him to see that the reader needs punctuation to show where there is a pause. Tell the student to pause every time he would naturally take a breath in his reading, and put a mark to indicate that this is where the full stops or commas should come.
- *Forming the sentences*: With a writer whose punctuation is weak, a good tip is to ask him to form each sentence in his head before it is written down. He can then work on one sentence at a time, adding full stops where necessary.
- *Punctuating dialogue*: The writer has also neglected to punctuate the speech. Ask him to underline or highlight the words in the passage that are actually spoken, to help with punctuating the dialogue.

Repetitive writing

Jamie climbed up into the cave. Then he took his torch out. Then he shone his torch around the cave. The cave was dark and Jamie couldn't see what was at the back. Then he walked to the back of the cave. When he got to the back of the cave he shone his torch again. When he did this he saw a big spider. When he saw the spider he got very scared. Then he ran out of the cave.

Diagnosis

This writing is very repetitive, and consequently sounds stilted. It is also dull for the reader, because of the lack of interest in the vocabulary. There is excessive use of the word 'then' – a fairly common problem for younger writers who are trying to divide their work up into sentences, and show the chain of events chronologically, but who are not yet using a sufficient variety of adverbs to show the time sequence.

Strategies

- *Identify the repetition*: Ask the child to underline any word that is repeated more than two times in the piece of writing. In this case, the words 'cave', 'then' and 'when'.

- *Look for alternatives*: Talk to the child about how a noun such as cave might be replaced by the word 'it'. Alternatively, it is often possible to remove the noun altogether, for instance in the sentence 'Then he shone his torch around the cave' the words 'the cave', could be completely removed. The sentence would still make sense, as the reader already knows where Jamie is.

- *Develop a bank of adverbs*: The writer here needs to find alternatives to the chain of 'thens' and 'whens'. At this stage, a bank of words which show a sequences of events would be useful: first, next, finally, and so on.

Irrelevant facts

Essay question: Discuss the characters of Macbeth and Lady Macbeth, exploring the relationship between them, and the way that this relationship changes during the course of the play.

Shakespeare was born in 1564 in Stratford-upon-Avon. He lived there before moving to London to work as an actor and writer. His play *Macbeth* is about a man called Macbeth who kills the king. The king's name is King Duncan. After he has killed King Duncan, Macbeth himself becomes king. Macbeth's wife is called Lady Macbeth.

Diagnosis

In this example of an essay introduction, the student begins with a list of facts, none of which have any relevance to the question that has been asked. This is typical of the essay writing produced by students who understand the story of a text, and who have listened to explanations of the historical background, and so on. However, there is little awareness here of what is required to answer an essay question, and very limited understanding of theme, character, etc.

Strategies

- *Teach the 'four-step' technique*: Use the 'four-step' essay writing technique described in Chapter 4 (pp.69–74). This will help the student to understand the steps of explanation and development that are required to gain marks.
- *Use the question to answer the question*: Encourage the student to start his essay by turning the question into a statement. This will help him stick to the point. In this example, he might write 'The characters Macbeth and Lady Macbeth have a very complex relationship.'
- *'Assumed knowledge'*: Remind the student that he can assume a certain amount of prior knowledge on the part of the person reading the essay. For instance, in this case it is safe to assume that the marker will know the names of the characters and their relationships to each other.

Listing

Essay question: Analyse the imagery used in the poem 'Upon Westminster Bridge' by William Wordsworth.

In 'Upon Westminster Bridge' Wordsworth uses lots of imagery. He uses lots of personification and similes. He personifies the city, saying that it 'wears' the beauty of the morning. He personifies the river, saying it 'glideth at his own sweet will'. He uses the simile 'like a garment' . . .

Diagnosis

Here, the student understands what imagery is, and is keen to show that she can identify examples of personification and similes. However, the problem is that the student does not understand what is meant by the word 'analyse'. Instead she lists the images that she has found, without explaining any of them, or offering any further development of the points. She is taking only the first two steps outlined in the 'four-step' writing technique (see Chapter 4).

Strategies

- *Explain the question vocabulary*: Talk to the student about how important it is to examine the vocabulary of the question. Here, the word 'analyse' is asking for a detailed examination of the use, effect and purpose of these images.
- *Teach steps 3 and 4*: Go over the third and fourth steps of the essay writing technique with the student. Show her how it is the explanation and development of a point that will gain her the marks.
- *Encourage one paragraph per point*: Ask the student to rewrite the essay, giving an entire paragraph to each example of imagery, by including an explanation and development of each point.

Part 4

Writing: Around the Subject

10 First steps to writing

When they start at school, our children are just stepping out on the long and complex journey to literacy. The first part of their journey involves the acquisition of physical, intellectual and emotional skills – the ability to put pen to paper and the desire and confidence to communicate their ideas. They must make the connection between sounds and their written form on the page, moving from writing letters, to words, to whole sentences.

This chapter explores ways in which teachers can help early and emerging writers to develop their work. I examine the skills and attitudes that go together to make a 'good' writer. I look at the steps that children take when they are first learning to write. I explore the acquisition and development of writing skills during the early part of the primary years: from the very first marks on the page, to the ability to form sentences and then paragraphs. Although the majority of the activities and approaches here will be of most use to primary school teachers, an awareness of how writing is acquired will be of benefit to teachers in the secondary school as well.

What makes a good writer?

Once the technical skills described in this book are in place, anyone will be able to write. Whether or not they become a good and effective writer is another matter. Right from the start, it is worth understanding the attributes and attitudes that a person needs in order to write well. Our aim should be to encourage these areas in our children from their very earliest attempts to write. The tips, advice and strategies given throughout this book will help you teach your students to become the best writers that they can possibly be. A good writer, of any age, will be someone who:

- Reads widely and frequently.
- Is motivated to communicate via the written word.
- Has an enjoyment of sounds, words and texts.
- Likes to look at texts, play with them, dig into them and analyse what is there.
- Reads with an understanding of how the writer works.
- Writes with an awareness of what will work for the reader.
- Has an ability to structure his or her ideas.
- Has an understanding of strategies connected to the technical side of writing.
- Can be both analytical and creative.

Reading and writing: the vital link

There is an absolutely crucial link between the dual literacy skills of reading and writing. As someone who writes for a living, I regularly devour at least three books a week, of all different types. This reading feeds constantly into my writing, and exactly the same applies for the children in your class. If you can get them reading as frequently and as widely as possible, you will inevitably help them become more effective writers. Here are some ideas about how you can encourage this constant reading.

- *Involve the parents*: We only see our children for a limited period during the week, and the demands of the curriculum mean that time spent on reading may be relatively brief. Explain the link between reading and literacy to your children's parents and find ways to encourage them to read regularly with their children at home.
- *Get them reading anything and everything*: The reading that your children do will take many forms – not just reading story books, but also reading magazines, posters, labels, and so on. In some ways, it really doesn't matter what the reading material is, or whether it is 'quality' writing or not. Even a badly written book will be giving its readers information about what does and does not work when it comes to their own writing.
- *Get them to see books as a natural part of life*: Children need to see books, and other forms of writing, as a normal part of life. If a child comes from a home where his parents read on a regular

basis, he will learn to see reading as a natural and enjoyable process. Similarly, in the classroom we can make books available and accessible for whenever there is a spare moment.

- *Teach them to read as a writer and write as a reader.* You will need to encourage your children to take this approach. Show them how to look at what has already been written and decide what does and does not work. With the very youngest children this might mean using class discussions of story books, or individual reviews of texts they have read. Similarly, encourage them to write with a sense of what their reader will appreciate, for instance reading their work out loud to the class and asking for feedback.

Speaking and writing: the weakest link?

At its heart, all writing is about communication. When I write, I type down the words that I might speak, although obviously with some editing and amendment. Writing is effectively like speaking to the reader via the written word. This link between speaking and writing can cause problems for those children who find it hard to articulate themselves properly. For example, I have noticed that my students often write 'would of' instead of 'would have' or 'would've'. What they are doing is writing as they speak. Similarly, if a child finds it hard to construct short, concise and clear sentences verbally, then this weakness will often be transmitted to the page.

Here are some tips that will help you develop your children's speaking skills, and consequently their written work.

- *Practice makes perfect*: Give your class lots of opportunities to speak in a range of different formats and a variety of forums. This could include:
  - Whole-class discussions
  - Circle time
  - Improvisations
  - In-role play
  - Games
  - Singing
  - Tape recordings
  - Videos

- *Develop their confidence*: Some of your children will lack confidence when it comes to speaking, especially in front of the whole class. You can help them develop more confidence by:
  - Building up slowly – gradually moving from group discussions to individual presentations.
  - Giving lavish praise – when a shy child does make an oral contribution, praise her to the skies.
  - Not rushing it – don't put your shy individuals on the spot: let them contribute in their own good time.
- *Make it fun*: Most children really enjoy speaking work. Make it fun for them by using props, costumes, games, and so on. The use of fictional approaches, such as role plays, is an excellent way of having fun with language.
- *Teach them how to structure speaking*: Advise your children about how to structure their spoken work. For instance, in a group task you might ask each child to contribute one idea in turn, before moving into a general discussion.
- *Explain formal/informal language*: You will need to advise your children about how to use the correct language for the relevant situation, encouraging them to think about audience expectations.
- *Develop Standard English*: As I noted above, your children will tend to write as they speak. If you want them to write 'properly' then you will need to teach them how to speak 'properly' as well.
- *Use lots of listening tasks*: Just as the avid reader will tend to write better, so the development of listening skills will feed into your children's speaking and writing work. Teach your children to listen by using a variety of listening activities on a daily basis. You might like to look at my book *Getting the Buggers to Think* (London: Continuum, 2003) for some ideas about developing listening skills.

Getting ready to write

From a very early stage, around two years old or even before, children will start to make marks on paper if given the relevant materials and guidance. It seems almost as though the urge to draw and write is hard-wired into our genetic make-up – as soon as our hands are ready to hold the writing materials, we can hardly wait to get going.

There is a certain magic about the very earliest part of the process of learning to write. In some ways, it's a mistake to over-analyse our students' first attempts at writing. Instead, it might be better for us to let this process happen organically. There is certainly no need to panic early on, and to try and force our children into writing before they are ready. A baby will become a toddler by walking when he or she feels physically and mentally ready, and when the motivation to move is strong. So, too, a child will write when he or she feels physically, mentally and emotionally ready to communicate via the written word.

Before they can even attempt to write properly, your children will need to have some very important skills and concepts under their belts. I've listed some of these areas below, divided up into the three main skill areas of physical, intellectual and psychological readiness.

- *Physical*: Once you know how to do it, writing is a very natural process, needing very little thought – a bit like riding a bicycle! However, right at the start our children need to have various physical skills under their belts. These include:
  - Holding a pen/pencil.
  - Using the pen to make marks on the paper.
  - Sitting at a table.
  - Hearing the sounds of words.
  - Concentrating for a length of time.
- *Intellectual/conceptual*: Again, the concepts about writing/ language that are vital to writing quickly become subconscious. Our youngest writers must understand:
  - How words are used to communicate meaning.
  - That certain letters make certain sounds.
  - That these sounds can be represented in writing.
  - That letters form words, and that these words can form sentences.
  - That we can communicate via the written word.
- *Psychological/emotional*: As well as being physically and

intellectually ready to write, our students must also over-come any fears that they have. They must be:
- Confident about expressing themselves.
- Happy to share their ideas with others.
- Unafraid of making mistakes or 'getting it wrong'.

The first steps

There are various ways that teachers can make the first steps to writing a positive experience. Many of the approaches described below will be just as relevant higher up the primary school and even into the secondary years.

- *Putting pen to paper*: Long before the youngest children are ready to start writing 'properly', they should be putting pen to paper on a regular basis. Even if they are only scribbling, the concepts that they can communicate by doing this will start to sink in. In addition, the act of scribbling will help them develop the dexterity they need in order to write.
- *Drawing as well as writing*: This dexterity can be developed by drawing and colouring activities, as well as by written ones. Use colouring-in, painting, join the dots and other drawing tasks to get your children comfortable with making marks on paper.
- *Getting the physical action right*: Encourage your youngest writers to hold the writing instrument in the correct way. You might use a manufactured pen-holder to make this easier for them, or perhaps mould some plasticine around the pen to make it easier to grip correctly.
- *Experimenting with different instruments*: Some children will find a chunky pen size easier to work with; others will prefer to write with a felt-tip rather than a pen or pencil. Experimenting to find the instrument that best suits each individual will help make the initial steps much more comfortable.
- *Making the materials attractive*: If the writing materials available are attractive, this will inevitably encourage the children to use them. This might mean providing brightly coloured pens and pencils, or a variety of sizes, types and colours of paper.

- *Seeing writing all around*: Our children need constant exposure to written texts if they are to understand the purpose and importance of writing. The teacher can help with this process by labelling items in the primary classroom, and by putting up lots of posters that use language.
- *Keeping it active*: Active learning will always be more enjoyable and memorable. For instance, when learning verbs you might call out the words and get your class to 'do' the actions.
- *A writing table*: You might like to provide a writing table where the children can scribble or write unsupervised. At the earliest stage, it is best that no one comments on or criticizes what the children produce at this table, so that they feel free to write without fear of getting it wrong.
- *Watching others write*: Your children will be seeing other people writing, particularly their teacher, whether this is on a blackboard, interactive whiteboard, or on their work. As you write, talk about what you are doing and the intellectual processes that are taking place.
- *'Writing' on the computer*: Writing on a computer will allow even the very youngest children to communicate through language. Although at this stage they might type little of real meaning, the very process of getting letters onto the page will be of benefit.
- *Keep it relevant and fun*: Right from the start, there is the danger that we might demotivate our young writers. Keep the work as fun and relevant as possible, for instance asking your children to write to persuade you to do something fun with the class.
- *Regular revisiting*: When you first begin to introduce new letters or words, make sure that you keep the new material minimal, and revisit each new area regularly. Rather than overloading your young children with lots to learn, it is better to ensure that the most commonly used letters, letter blends and words are in place.

Letter activities

Once we move onto the actual formation of letters, there is the danger we might focus heavily on writing practice. Keeping the work active and imaginative will help your children to acquire and remember these new letters and will also show them that writing can be fun. The key skills for early letter activities are to understand the shapes and sound of each letter, and also to focus on the correct direction for writing them down.

- *Body shapes*: When you first introduce a new letter, get the children to make the letter shape with their bodies. They might do this individually (for a 'T') or in pairs (for an 'M').
- *Letters in the air*: Similarly, get your children drawing letters in the air with their hands, focusing on the correct direction in which to write. You will need to stand with your back to the class to show them how to do this.
- *Letter focus*: Spend a day or more focusing on one regularly used letter, doing lots of activities related to it. For instance, you might spend time making pictures of the letter, or finding lots of words that start with this letter.
- *Big letters*: Making something big is always very appealing. Get your children to write huge letters, for example drawing them in chalk on the playground floor.
- *What starts with?*: Ask your class to list all the words they can think of that start with a specified letter. The children could call these out while the teacher writes them down. You might set up a competition to see which child or group can find the most words that start with this letter.
- *'Blind' letters*: Get your children to close their eyes, and then trace the shape of a letter on the palm of their hand. This exercise could also be done in pairs, with the children tracing the letter shapes on their partner's back.
- *Sculpted letters*: Set your class an activity to make letters out of plasticine or any other suitable material. You could then make a display of all the different sculptures.
- *Letter collage*: Give your children a big stack of magazines, and then ask them to find all the images that start with a particular letter. They could then move on to make a collage of images that all start with the same letter of the alphabet.
- *'I spy'*: 'I spy' is a great game for working on letters – you

might set this up as a group task or work with the whole class at once.

- *Letter families*: Spend time looking at letters which have a similar shape, for example 'o', 'd' and 'p'. These similar-looking letters can often be a source of difficulty for early writers, so try to find ways to help them remember the differences.
- *Time for assimilation*: It is a good idea to introduce only a few letters at a time, then to give the children a chance to assimilate what they have learned. For instance, after some active work they might spend some time doing a quiet task, such as colouring in letter shapes.
- *Phonic approaches*: As well as learning the shapes of the letters, your children will also need to learn the sounds that these letters can make. You might use some chants or songs to help your children practise the sounds of different letters.
- *Letter blends*: Once several letters have been learned, your class can move on to blending these letters together, looking at the different words and sounds that can be made in this way. Many of the letter activities described above can also be used for creating letter blends.

From letters to words

Your children will soon have a few letters, and letter blends, under their belts. They can then move on to creating words. Below are a number of ideas for fun and engaging word activities.

- *Scrabble*: Get some letter tiles, either from a game of Scrabble or ones made by the class. Now call out a word to the class and ask them to make this word using the letters. This might be done individually or in groups. You could also give your children around five letter tiles of commonly used letters. They could then see how many words they can make out of these letters.
- *Unjumble the letters*: Give your children short words with the letters jumbled up, perhaps with a picture to help them work out the answer. They should then unjumble these letters to make a word, for example tca becomes 'cat'.

- *Word searches*: Word searches offer an excellent way of working with, and searching for, words, and also looking at letter patterns. Children do seem to love doing word searches, and they offer an excellent, quiet focused activity.
- *Circle words*: Get your class to sit in a circle. Start by giving a word, for example 'elephant'. The next person in the circle must now come up with a word that starts with the last letter of the word just given. So, the second person might say 'tomato', the next person 'orange', and so on. You might set a particular topic for this, or just allow the class to free associate as they wish. This activity could also be done in small groups.
- *Active verbs*: Introduce verbs in an active way, talking to your class about how these are 'doing' words. Get your children to come up in front of the class and 'do' an action, then ask the others to identify which verb fits the action. One child might come up and show 'swim', another 'jump', and so on.
- *Early strategies*: Right from the earliest possible opportunity, start to give your children the strategies that they will need to help them with spelling. Look at how words with the same letter blends will have similar sounds, for example, 'cat', 'hat' and 'sat'. Chapter 2 gives you lots of ideas for helping your children to develop their own ways of remembering spellings, and many of these can be adapted to use with the very youngest writers.
- *Naming language*: At this stage your children should be hearing you use linguistic terminology, although obviously at the very simplest level. Words such as 'noun' and 'verb' can become part of the everyday language of the classroom, gradually leading onto more complex grammatical terminology.

From words to sentences

Once your children have mastered a sufficient range of vocabulary, they will be ready to start forming sentences. These two processes (learning how to spell words, creating sentences) will be happening simultaneously. At the most basic level, all the children really need to construct a sentence is knowledge of subjects and verbs, so that they can write 'The girl jumps'. At this stage, the complex structures they are using in their spoken language, and seeing in their reading, will start to translate onto the page.

You can find lots of ideas for working on the basic techniques (spelling, punctuation, grammar, etc.) in Chapter 2. Here are a couple of ideas for starting out on sentence work.

Playing the part

Create grammatically correct sentences, with the children playing the different types of word. For instance, one child could act out the subject of the sentence (for example, pretending to be a cat), while another acts out the verb (for example, sitting down). This could lead to the construction of sentences such as 'The cat sits.' Develop these sentences by asking for a location, such as 'on the mat' or 'on a cushion'.

Who/what/where?

To help your children construct simple sentences, you might like to play a game of 'who/what/where?'. Give the class a series of pictures and ask:

- Who is it?
- What is it doing?
- Where is it?

From these three questions, your children can construct sentences such as:

- The girl/stands/in the classroom.
- A girl/sits/in the chair.
- The cat/walks/on the table.
- A cat/plays/in the garden.

This game can be developed to use different grammatical constructions. So, to work on adverbs you might ask who/what/how instead, with the third question being 'How is it doing it?' The answers could include:

- The dog runs quickly.
- The girl eats slowly.

Motivation for early writers

Once your children have got up a head of steam, and are writing in full sentences, it is important to make sure that their motivation remains high. At this point, those who struggle to express themselves through writing are in danger of slipping into disaffection. If we can find ways to avoid this at the earliest stage, we should hopefully be able to keep our young writers keen on the process of writing.

- *Use resources to inspire them*: Asking your children to write about something concrete is a sure-fire way to inspire them. Give them a huge empty box and ask them to write about what it once contained, or what might be built from it. Show them a variety of shells and ask them to write about the exotic beach where these were found.
- *Still-life*: Looking in detail at an object encourages early writers to develop their descriptive powers. Give your children a set of objects and ask them to write about what they see, or perhaps to explore the different connections and associations that might be made by using these objects.
- *Use non-written approaches*: At the start of our writing careers, it can be frustrating to express ourselves because we lack a range of vocabulary. Rather than focusing solely on writing, include other approaches that allow your children to express themselves fully. This might mean:
  - Tape-recording a story and writing out small segments of this.
  - Getting the children to tell the class about their week-ends, and showing them how key words from their account are spelt.
- *Use collaborative approaches*: Working as part of a team will help students with weaker literacy skills to succeed. Your children might work in groups to write a letter, or they could work as a whole class to create a story.
- *Don't overcorrect*: We need to strike a balance between correcting our children's work, and cramping their style at an early stage. Take a variety of approaches to marking – at times looking in detail at correct spelling or punctuation, at other times praising content over form.

- *Use a variety of forms*: Get your class working with a variety of forms – some of which they will be familiar with, and others that they have less experience of using. Include some forms that do not require the use of full sentences, for instance:
  - Recipes
  - Lists
  - Emails
  - Text messages
  - Postcards
- *Give structures and frames*: At this stage, your children will not yet have mastered the skill of structuring their writing. You can help them to do this by giving a frame for their work related to the form being used, whether this is a letter, a story, a postcard, etc. This frame would include the correct layout and some key vocabulary for their writing.
- *Fill in the blanks*: To develop simultaneously the skills of reading and writing, you might like to give your children some writing with various words left out. They could then work, individually or in groups, to fill in the blanks. This might mean giving a story with some words missing, for example, 'The ... ran down the road to catch the ...', and so on.

11 Writing for all

Our aim as teachers is to get *all* our students to learn to write, and preferably to learn to write well. If they don't succeed in this challenge, they will be handicapped for the rest of their lives. Those who are not fully literate are restricted in the type of employment they can find when they leave school. They are also limited in their ability to communicate via the written word, whether in a letter, an email, or a job application. We owe it to all our children to develop their writing to the best of our (and their) ability. This chapter examines how we might achieve this: for the least able and the gifted, the boys as well as the girls, those for whom English is a second language and those who find it difficult to behave themselves.

Helping the least able

I can imagine that it must be hugely frustrating for those children who find writing a real challenge. Day after day they arrive at school, knowing all too well that they are going to have to write in the vast majority of their lessons. It is hardly surprising that some of these children only enjoy the practical subjects, such as PE, drama and art. At least in these areas they can communicate their ideas and complete the activities without the challenge of having to write. It also does not surprise me that these students will often lose their focus during lesson time and resort to misbehaviour. This may be as a result of their embarrassment in finding a relatively simple task so challenging. In order to hide their discomfort, they play the 'class clown' or give the teacher a hard time.

Here are some thoughts about how you can help those children who find writing a challenge equal to scaling Mount Everest.

- *Don't believe the worst*: It can be tempting to make negative judgements of your least able students. The frustration of repeatedly being presented with poor pieces of writing can make you believe that these students are simply not putting any effort into their work. While this might be true for a minority, do try to assume that your children have tried their hardest, while insisting that they strive to achieve better results next time. If there are children who present you with poor writing on a regular basis, ensure that a special needs teacher has assessed them to check for learning difficulties.

- *Stay positive*: Try to retain a positive approach, looking for what *has* worked in the writing rather than focusing on what hasn't. It could be that your weakest writers have excellent and imaginative ideas, and it is merely the technique that prevents you from appreciating this. While I am not suggesting that you should praise poor work, be aware that these children will be faced with negativity and failure day after day, and that this cycle needs to be broken.

- *Watch your language*: Do take care over what you say to your least able children. When you are tired or stressed, it is all too easy to throw off a casual comment, such as 'this is terrible – you haven't made much effort with it, have you?' The child could take this type of comment very personally indeed. Writing is an expression of who we are, and it is hard for writers of any age to accept criticism of their work. Try to phrase your criticisms in a constructive way, identifying something that the child has done well (even if this is as simple as putting a title on the work).

- *Set them targets*: Everyone needs something to strive for, but for the weak writer it may feel like there's so much that needs putting right that there's no point in even trying. We can help our weak children develop their writing by setting small, achievable targets, and rewarding them when these targets are met. For instance, you might ask a child to aim for the neatest handwriting that she can produce, and reward good effort with a sticker.

- *Give them a break*: Give the weakest writers a break from writing on occasions, especially those for whom the technical demands prove very stressful. This break might involve:

- *The use of a scribe*: This could be the class teacher, a learning assistant, or even another child. Having a scribe to write down what the child says allows him to focus on the content of his work, rather than worrying about technique.
- *The use of a tape recorder*: Talking into a tape recorder will help the child to develop oral skills, and to focus on developing the content of her work, without worrying about the need to spell, write neatly, and so on. After making the recording, the child could choose one part of her work to write out.
- *The use of a computer*: For children whose handwriting is very weak, using a computer gives a welcome break. If you have access to a portable computer, your least able writers might use this on a regular basis in the classroom.
- *Use group activities*: For the least able, working as part of a group offers a welcome relief from the stress of individual writing. In a mixed-ability setting, the more able children will often help their less able counterparts to succeed. In addition, the least able can choose to complete those tasks that are best suited to their own talents, for instance drawing or design work.

Extending the gifted writer

At the opposite end of the spectrum from the least able are the 'gifted and talented' children, and some of these students will indeed be exceptional writers. It is hard to offer challenges to those at the top end of the ability range in a mixed-ability classroom, while still giving the opportunity for the rest of the children to succeed. Set extension activities whenever possible, and give homework tasks that build on the work done in class to stretch your most able writers. The ideas below give you some thoughts about how this can be done.

- *Work on their 'voice'*: One of the most complex aspects of being a writer is finding and maintaining your own personal writing style or 'voice'. Encourage your students to hear this voice internally as they work, listening to the writing in their heads, simultaneously reading and writing. Developing a 'voice' might mean adding splashes of humour or informality to the work, or adapting the way punctuation and italics are used to give emphasis. A good way of developing your own voice as a writer is to practice 'echoing' the voice that other writers use, for instance writing a detective story 'in the style of' Elmore Leonard or Raymond Chandler.

- *Use rewriting activities*: A useful exercise for able students is rewriting the work of other authors in a different style. This might mean reworking a broadsheet newspaper article into the style of a tabloid; turning an adult story into one for children; or changing a formal letter into an informal one. As they do this, students will need to adapt the vocabulary, style, etc., as appropriate, learning about the different aspects that make up a good piece of writing.

- *Use analysis activities*: A good way of developing our students' knowledge about writing and language is for them to analyse the way that other writers work. This knowledge can then be adapted and applied to their own writing. For instance, they might look at how writers in different genres structure their sentences to create a sense of pace and rhythm, and to develop tension. They could look for the use of language devices within a text and consider the effects that these create. The best writers are often the most avid readers, and your talented students are probably subconsciously analysing the books that they read already.

- *Develop linguistic techniques*: Able students should be capable, from a very young age, of using imagery and other linguistic techniques in their work. Don't be afraid to introduce these techniques early on, either on an individual or a whole-class basis. Your students might use repetition to emphasize a point; they could use an extended metaphor to give their work a sense of style; they might use alliteration to create a more interesting sound for the reader. These techniques can be used right across the curriculum, not just in English lessons.

- *Develop the use of punctuation*: Encourage your very able students to explore a more advanced use of punctuation. For instance, teach them when it is appropriate to use a colon or semicolon, and the syntactical rules behind this.

- *Break the rules*: Students who are very able in the technique of writing may need to learn how to bend the rules once in a while. The 'best' writers are not merely technically accurate, but also need imagination and a willingness to experiment. The more conscious this bending of the rules is, the better it will work. Rather than simply making mistakes, bending the rules shows that a writer has complete control of his writing style. For instance, your students might play with grammar to create a sense of personal style, perhaps splitting the odd infinitive when they feel it is appropriate. They could use the conjunctions 'and' or 'but' to start a sentence, in order to create a better sound, flow or pace in their writing.
- *Develop vocabulary*: Make sure that the most able writers have access to a thesaurus, whether in a book or on the computer. This will help them to develop a wider vocabulary, and to consider a range of words, picking out the one that is most appropriate to the context and sound of what they are writing. Encourage them to explore the definition of unfamiliar words, using a dictionary to consider the subtle variations of meaning that are available.
- *Think about sound*: The best writers consider the sound of the words that they use, as well as their meaning. Encourage your students to consider the way their language would sound when read out loud by hearing their writing in their heads. Also, ask them to think about how words with different sounds might add interest to their work.
- *Encourage a sense of self*: As well as having their own voice, good writers put a sense of themselves into their work. This might mean offering an emotional response to a subject, or referring to personal experiences to back up the point being made.
- *Encourage intertextual reference*: As their work becomes more complex, able writers should be encouraged to look for other texts to refer to in their writing. Intertextual reference might involve quoting an acknowledged expert on a subject, or it could mean referring to a link that the student has discovered between one novel or author and another.

Boys and writing

There has been much debate about why boys are less successful in their writing than girls. Part of the problem is perhaps our own perceptions as teachers of the ways in which boys write. This, however, is a book of ideas and strategies and consequently not the place for a debate about this issue. Rather, I would like to offer some practical tips that have worked for me in the classroom for developing boys' writing. You might feel that what follows is rather stereotyped and generalized. However, these ideas all arise from my own classroom experience – my goal is to offer you ideas that will work, rather than to be politically correct. Many of these tips will work as well with girls as they do with boys.

- *Consider quality v. quantity*: Some boys turn out shorter pieces of writing than their female classmates, and the natural tendency is for us to make a judgement based on quantity as well as quality. However, the best and most effective pieces of writing are often very concise. When marking and assessing work, try to consider whether the boys in your class achieve as much as the girls, but simply using less words.
- *Consider presentation v. content*: Similarly, you might find that your male students do not present their work in as attractive a way as their female counterparts. Again, look at the quality of the content rather than allowing the appearance of the writing to sway your judgement.
- *Be gender-neutral*: The majority of primary school teachers are female, and our gender surely affects our perceptions of written work. Men and women tend to have different priorities in their reading interests, and in what they view as 'good' writing. When you read and mark your students' work do try hard to judge it from a 'gender-neutral' position.
- *Find out what inspires them*: Certain genres appeal strongly to boys, typically science fiction, fantasy and horror. Find out which areas of fiction appeal to the boys that you teach and capitalize on their interests. Encourage them to read within these genres as well, as this will inevitably have a positive impact on their writing. If you do have reluctant older

readers in your class, why not offer them a book of short stories? Alternatively, even reading comics or magazines is better than nothing.

- *Use the media*: In my experience, media-based writing is very popular with boys, so try to incorporate media forms into at least some of your lessons. Reading magazines is a popular activity with boys, and teachers can utilize this interest to engage them, for instance by setting up a project to produce a magazine. Writing and videotaping scripts, or basing written work on films and television, can also lead to high levels of enthusiasm.

- *Use group projects*: My classroom experience suggests that boys produce good work when they are given a group project to do, especially one that covers a topic of interest to them (football, computer games and wrestling spring to mind). The talents of our students lie in many different areas of the wide field of 'writing', and a group project allows each person to bring their own talents to the task.

- *Use computer games*: Many computer games contain a very strong (and sequenced) narrative that can be useful in helping your students to write stories. Talk to your students about the games that they play on their computers, and analyse the way the narrative is structured within these games.

- *Use visualization*: Ask your students to visualize each part of a story, either viewing it as a movie in their heads, or drawing up a storyboard of the sequence of events that take place. The ability to develop a sequence of events plays an important part in good story writing.

- *Action v. description*: On the whole, boys seem to enjoy and succeed in writing action-based pieces, while girls tend more towards the descriptive. When setting a subject for class writing, offer a few different topics, some which lend themselves to descriptive writing and others that lean more towards action.

- *'Slugs and snails!!!'*: Being asked to write about something disgusting will motivate many of our students, whether they are boys or girls. This might be writing about a repulsive alien who comes to Earth, it could be drawing and labelling a design of the most hideous-looking monster in the Universe, it might be writing a recipe for the most disgusting cake ever made.

Teaching students with ESL/EAL

Teaching students whose first language is not English can be very rewarding. They are generally very keen to learn and to work, and they also bring with them to the classroom a huge range of cultural and life experiences that differ from the 'norm'. The majority of us have only ever learnt a second language at school, and then only for a relatively short space of time. However, these bi- or trilingual children have the advantage of being completely immersed in the English language, at least during the course of the school day. Although we may feel that they are slow to pick up the words at first, eventually this immersion will lead to a far greater and deeper knowledge of their new language. Here are some tips and thoughts about working with children who have English as a second or additional language. Many of these ideas are taken from my experience of working in a multilingual international school.

- *Grammatical understanding*: The difference between the structure of their mother tongue and of the English language will often result in grammatical errors, for instance in the placement of verbs within a sentence. It is worth taking time to teach a child with ESL about word order and other areas of English grammar.
- *Grammatical awareness*: You can help both the child and your class as a whole by developing their grammatical awareness. For instance, you might look at the way in which regular verbs are conjugated in English. This would also help the other students in your class become more aware of how their own language works.
- *Irregular verbs*: These can be very confusing for ESL children. It is a good idea to give them lists of how to conjugate the most commonly used irregular verbs, such as 'to be'.
- *A two-way learning process*: Widen your own knowledge by asking an ESL child to teach you some words in his

language. Helping out his teacher offers a wonderful way of making the child feel a bit 'special'.

- *Make the child an expert*: If the child is confident enough, ask him to share a few words of his language with the class. He might teach the numbers from one to ten, the days of the week, or different parts of the body. You may be surprised how receptive children are to learning another language (especially the younger ones), and you can have some great fun at the same time. By sharing his expertise the child will feel that he has an important contribution to make to the class as a whole.

- *Give them key vocabulary*: Give the ESL child a list of key terms or technical words in all the subjects of the curriculum. You might also give lists of these subject-specific words (mainly nouns) to the whole class. The children who already speak English could learn them as spellings, while the ESL child could learn them as new vocabulary. She could then play 'teacher' and read out the spellings for a spelling test.

- *Give the child a translator*: If you have two children in your class who have the same mother tongue, but who are at different stages in their acquisition of English, you might ask one of them to act as a translator for the other.

- *Be aware of cultural differences*: Language divides us because we cannot understand each other, but it also divides us at a cultural level. Be aware of, or even learn about, the type of culture from which your ESL students come, and how this might affect them within the classroom. For instance, the use of irony is prevalent in the English language, but many other cultures find it hard to understand, and consequently do not 'get' our humour. To give another example, some languages are written in a way that we would consider to be 'back to front', i.e. from right to left on the page, and from the back of a book to the front.

- *Work with texts from other countries*: Try to incorporate some texts from other countries and cultures into your classroom, whether in the original language or in translation (or even both). Doing this could provide you with some excellent written work with a multicultural basis.

- *Find out about other countries*: You might also set a project on the child's homeland as part of your class work. This could be especially effective in the primary school, or in geography lessons. If the child is willing, you could ask her to be an 'expert', talking to the class about what her country of origin is like.

Writing and behaviour

For some children, writing is difficult or impossible because they simply cannot behave themselves. This might be because of a lack of concentration or because they get involved in low-level misbehaviour, such as chatting and getting out of their seats. If this is the case with one or more of your students, your first priority must be to ensure good behaviour from all of your class. Here are a few tips that will help you get your children behaving properly, so that they can write to the best of their ability.

- *Set your boundaries*: When you set boundaries for your class, make it clear how written work will take place. If your boundaries are made sufficiently explicit from the start, your students will soon learn that this is the way they must work. Your boundaries should be both for behaviour during writing, and also for the quality and quantity of work that you expect to receive.
- *Explain your aims*: Set out the aims of the lesson clearly for your students, to 'signpost' the learning that is going to take place. Your children will feel much more secure, and have a much greater sense of purpose, if this is done at the start of every lesson.
- *Always be polite*: Be polite in the way you interact with your children, and also in the way that you react to their work. While it can be tempting to 'slag off' a piece of writing that you feel is of poor quality, this may be extremely destructive and demotivating to a child, especially to a child who finds writing difficult. In addition, you may encourage poor behaviour if the child feels his efforts are not valued. If you feel that a poor piece of work is a result of laziness, rather than weakness, you can still react politely and constructively.

For instance, you might say 'I just know you can do much better than this' rather than 'This is an awful piece of writing'.

- *Set individual targets*: Targets are extremely useful for individual students who find writing difficult. Ensure that the targets you set are high but realistic, and think about how many targets to give at any one time. It is always better to set a single specific target, such as 'put a full stop at the end of every sentence', rather than a generalized target or set of targets such as 'get your punctuation and spelling right'.
- *Set whole-class targets*: A great idea for setting whole-class targets is to divide the work up into:
  - The work that *must* be done.
  - The work that *should* be done.
  - And the work that *could* be done.

  By dividing the work into these three categories, the teacher sets clear boundaries for what must be completed. The more able students will stretch themselves by aiming for all three targets. The less able will retain a sense of achievement by completing the first two.
- *Use repetition*: Many times a teacher will explain a task only to find that, a few minutes later, several hands go up from students saying 'I don't understand what we're meant to do'. Use repetition when setting written work to clarify what must be done. After explaining the task, ask one of your students to repeat back to you the work that has been set. In this way you can clear up any misunderstandings at an early stage.
- *Know when to be flexible*: At certain times of the day or week, or under certain conditions that are out of your control, your students may not be in the right mood to write. A class returning from a lively PE lesson may find it very hard to settle down to written work; on a wet Friday afternoon, your students might achieve little of real value if they are asked to do an extended piece of writing. Know when to be flexible, and when practical work, speaking tasks or reading are more appropriate than writing. Better to be realistic than to struggle with your children, forcing them to write, creating a sense of resentment, and achieving little of real value.

- *Teaching styles*: For those students with poor concentration, or in a class where there is quite a lot of bad behaviour, we need to think carefully about suiting our teaching style to the children. Some ways that you might do this include:
  - Beginning the lesson with a fast-paced 'starter activity' to encourage students with a lack of focus to get into the mood for writing.
  - Starting each lesson in a similar manner to give a clear structure to the work.
  - Not teaching from the front for an entire lesson, especially with a class that tends to drift off-task easily.
  - Setting short targets, and rewarding the completion of each part of the work.
  - Using a range of activities that work for children with different learning styles – including active, hands-on work as well as more concentrated writing tasks.
- *Developing focus*: To write well, we need to be able to focus on the task at hand. If your students have poor concentration, and cannot stick at a written task for a long period of time, use some of the focus exercises described in Chapter 1 to develop their concentration.

12 Writing and ICT

For some people, writing on a computer seems almost like 'cheating'. There is a feeling that computers make the writer lazy, that they do the work for us, checking our spelling and grammar or offering us an electronic thesaurus when we can't find the right word. I would never suggest that computers could or should replace the need for our children to learn the techniques of writing. However, we should not be afraid to embrace the advantages that using ICT can bring, while bearing in mind its disadvantages.

This chapter looks at the ways in which ICT can be used to motivate your children and develop their writing. It explores the advantages and disadvantages of using computers as a teaching tool, and it also looks at resources such as the internet and email. As a writer and teacher, I make daily use of ICT, both inside and outside the classroom. My books are produced on a computer from the very first words to the final layout and submission. I also do much of my research on the internet, and I am in daily contact with other teachers and writers via email. As I said in the introduction to this book, the increasing use of technology means that writing becomes ever *more* important, and not less. The internet allows people from all over the world to publish their ideas and their writing in a public forum for anyone to access.

When you are using ICT in the classroom, bear in mind that your students (however young they are) may well know more about computers than you do. Today's children have grown up with technology, whereas some teachers might not have been taught to use even the most basic computers during their own schooling. Utilize the knowledge that your students have, and if there are experts on different aspects of ICT in your classroom, get them to help teach both you and the rest of your class.

Writing on a computer

Advantages

The secret of effective ICT use in the classroom is to consider the advantages that it brings, and to maximize these for our students. It is tempting to see the wordprocessor as merely a presentational tool, especially if you are not particularly computer-literate. However, its use goes way beyond simply producing 'pretty' pieces of work.

- *A building tool*: Wordprocessing software offers the writer a wonderful degree of flexibility. You can build a basic outline of a piece first, then fill in the gaps bit by bit, elaborating on each idea in turn. This initial outline can act as a useful plan, indicating the order in which the ideas will come, where the paragraph breaks should be, and so on.
- *An editing tool*: Wordprocessors allow us to edit our work with remarkable ease. We can cut out whole sections, move a paragraph from the beginning to the end of a piece of writing, change single words, alter sentence structure, and so on, all without taking much effort or time. Before the invention of the computer, such changes would have meant hours of work in rewriting by hand.
- *A presentational device*: Producing a finished and beautifully presented piece of writing can be highly motivating for children. Good presentation is also very pleasing for teachers and parents, and is useful when you want to display your students' writing. Presenting work on the computer is not just about printing out beautifully wordprocessed written assignments; it can also encompass the use of programs such as Powerpoint, which allow children to create a 'live' presentation of their writing.
- *Presenting worksheets*: Computers also offer an excellent way for teachers to present their own worksheets. Time spent on creating engaging and exciting worksheets can be very useful in motivating your students. Because copying and editing are so easy, we can make minor changes to differentiate these worksheets. A worksheet stored on the computer can also be easily accessed, updated, and printed out.

- *Help for those with SEN*: Using computers to write can be an excellent way of motivating those children who have special needs. For instance, a child who finds spelling incredibly difficult can have his worries eased by the use of a spell-checker.
- *Help with technical accuracy*: Computers allow us to write with a high degree of technical accuracy. Although computers should not replace the need for learning proper technique, spelling- and grammar-checkers provide a useful tool for identifying areas of difficulty.
- *Help for those with poor handwriting*: Writing on a computer can be helpful to those who find neat or legible handwriting a challenge. Again, although the teacher clearly needs to work with these children on developing and improving their handwriting, using a computer allows them to produce and present a piece of 'finished' work.

The disadvantages

Just as we should learn to maximize the advantages of computers for written tasks, so we also need to be aware of the disadvantages. By being conscious of these, we can take steps to avoid the potential pitfalls.

- *The potential for distraction*: When using a computer, it is easy to get distracted from the task in hand. For instance, there are so many different websites available on the internet, and it is so easy to click from one link to another, that a substantial amount of time can go by without anything concrete actually being achieved. Similarly, many children spend a lot of time playing with different fonts and text colours, rather than concentrating on the content of their writing.
- *The potential for laziness*: Although spelling- and grammar-checkers can be very useful, there is the potential for children to use them mindlessly, without considering why and where they are making mistakes.
- *An easy sense of achievement*: Computers can give a sense that you have achieved something simply because the work looks good. Teachers, as well as students, need to be aware that

content is what really matters, no matter how beautifully presented the piece of work might be.

- *The potential for plagiarism*: Electronic encyclopaedias and, of course, the internet make it annoyingly easy for students to 'cheat' in their writing. Fortunately, this plagiarism is often easy to spot, because the child does not make any attempt to hide the original source.

- *Computers never lie*: Technology can seduce us into feeling that everything we read on-screen is the 'truth'. This applies particularly to the internet – it is easy to be convinced that websites are factual and accurate, while this may not necessarily be true. Wordprocessing programs are often set up to offer American spelling and grammar, although this can easily be switched to the English version.

- *Sometimes we need to break the rules*: Sometimes writers will break grammatical rules on purpose, perhaps to achieve a certain tone or effect in their writing. If we rely totally on what a grammar-check tells us, we narrow down the possibilities for 'breaking the rules' and consequently for achieving some more interesting effects in our writing.

- *Availability of resources*: Many teachers face a situation where there are just not enough machines available, or where access to the internet is poor because of high levels of usage at certain times of the day. These factors need to be taken into account when planning for ICT work.

- *Over-editing*: Although one of the wonderful aspects of using a computer is the ability to edit without hours of rewriting by hand, this aspect also has its downside, in that it is often *too* easy for our students to edit their work. They go on and on fiddling with the piece, long beyond the point at which improvements are being made. With every piece of writing, there must come a point at which it is 'finished'.

- *'Typing up'*: There is always the temptation to use wordprocessing programs for 'typing up' handwritten pieces of work, rather than as a tool for building pieces of writing.

- *The '10 per cent rule'*: The majority of us (me included) use only a fraction of the functions available in our software programs. There are many tools of which we remain completely oblivious, probably because many of us learn 'on the job' and are not specifically trained in ICT.

Potential computing hazards

The 'hazards' listed below range from the light-hearted to the potentially serious. They are all problems that I have experienced during my time as a teacher, and I do have to admit a certain admiration for the huge range of potential problems my students seem able to dream up. (I must at least pay tribute to their ingenuity!) Below are some of the problems that I have encountered in the past, and suggestions for overcoming some of these issues.

- *Print-out mania*: Many is the time that I have faced the problem of a printer with a huge quantity of print jobs backed up on it, each one a single page sent by the same student. This is the student who simply refuses to believe that either (a) her work will eventually come out of the printer, or (b) one copy of her work is sufficient. There are several methods you could use to overcome this problem:
  - Explain to your children that once they have sent a page to the printer, it is stored in the printer's buffer memory. It will be printed eventually, and definitely does not need to be sent time and time again.
  - Although it is useful to encourage your students to use the 'Ctrl' functions as a shortcut, insist that they use the full process with the pull-down menus when printing a document.
  - Insist that your students ask permission before they send anything to print.
  - If they refuse to go along with this, simply turn the printer off!
- *ClipArt crazy*: For children, there is apparently something magical about having pictures available to add into their work. This use of ClipArt can be problematic for a number of reasons:
  - Pictures often take a long time to send and print out. The consequent wait can lead to a whole class full of panicking

children, sending the same pages to the printer over and over again, convinced that their work is not going to appear.

- ClipArt pictures use up huge quantities of ink from the printer cartridge, thus making for a very expensive visit to the computer room.
- Time spent fiddling around with pictures, or searching through the picture library for a suitable image, will often be at the expense of the content of the written work.

- *Crashing computers*: Considering the amount of use (and often abuse) that school computers suffer, it is surprising that they don't crash more often than they do. However, a computer crashing before a child has saved his work can cause real difficulty and stress for the student and for the teacher.

- *Internet connection problems*: Think about possible connection problems when you plan to use the internet in your teaching. There is nothing more frustrating than planning a lesson based on visiting various websites, only to find that your children cannot access them. The level of difficulty will vary according to the way that your school actually accesses the internet, and how the network (if there is one) is set up. The time of most difficulty seems to be mid-afternoon, when America 'logs on'.

- *Hidden windows*: The Windows operating system has a function that allows the user to have various documents and programs open at the same time, in different 'windows'. If you open a document in Windows and then minimize it (a button with a single dash at the top right of the screen) you will notice that it 'hides' at the bottom. Keep an eye out for these hidden windows when your children are using computers. The devious among them may be logging into chatrooms or onto their favourite websites when you are not looking, and then minimizing these as soon as they see you coming so that they can pretend to be working.

- *The disappearing mouse-ball*: If you have not yet experienced the disappearing mouse-ball trick, then be aware that inside the mouse is a small ball, about the size of a gobstopper, which can be easily removed. Ask each student to turn his or her mouse upside down at the end of the lesson, so that you can check whether all the balls are still in place.

- *Swapping the keys*: When I encountered this one I was truly amazed: in fact I didn't know whether to laugh or to cry! Basically, it is not difficult to pull the keys away from the keyboard and then swap them about. The next person to use the computer will be thoroughly confused when their typing does not seem to be coming out as it should!

- *Fingers, fingers everywhere*: There seems to be an attraction for some children in putting their fingers into every possible area of the computer, including the CD-ROM, disk drives and electrical connections. This is not only dangerous, but is also potentially damaging to the computer. If you experience this behaviour from your students, the simple answer is to ban them from using the machines until they can treat them with the respect they deserve.

- *The big freeze*: Spend some time explaining to your students what they should do if the computer crashes. The automatic reaction seems to be to turn the computer off at the mains, but if they do this the machines may be damaged. For those of you who do not already know, the best thing is to hit the Ctrl, Alt and Delete buttons simultaneously, which will (almost always) reboot the computer.

- *Safety on the internet*: I have devoted a whole section to this issue below, as it is now a really crucial issue for ICT use. Many of us are just beginning to see the classroom potential, both good and bad, that the internet offers. We need to develop an awareness of safety issues as soon as possible – after all, the children in our class are our responsibility. If we are going to introduce them to the world of the web, we need to ensure that they are properly equipped to deal with it.

Common wordprocessing errors

Written work will generally take place using a wordprocessing program, and it is therefore sensible to consider some of the more common errors that your students might make, and how these might be avoided. Although they are relatively simple things, the errors listed below are ones that I have seen from countless numbers of students. It really is worth spending the first lesson or two on computers teaching the whole class how to use the functions correctly.

- *Space-bar fever*: The student with 'space-bar fever' fails to make any use of the left/right and centre alignment functions. They also completely ignore the tab button. Over the years I have watched many students with their thumbs pressed hard down on the space bar in order to centre or right align their text. Do explain to them how simple the computer makes it for us to layout our work.
- *Wrap around*: Similarly, I have been presented with strange looking pieces of writing, in which the student has used the return key at the end of a line, rather than allowing the text to wrap around automatically. This might not be apparent at first glance, but soon becomes a problem when the student edits the work and the new lines appear in the middle of the page.
- *New page*: In Microsoft Word, the shortcut for adding a new page is Ctrl+Return. Your students may instead simply add a number of returns in order to move onto a new page – a mistake that only becomes obvious when they try to change the order of their writing.
- *Blank pages*: When checking through a student's work before it is sent to print, I have often come across a series of blank pages at the end of a document. My theory is that these appear because the student overuses the return key (see above). Do encourage your students to delete these blank pages before printing – otherwise you will find hundreds of clear white sheets spewing out of the printer.
- *What's in a name?*: The name that they give their documents might seem trivial to your students, but there is nothing more frustrating than not being able to find that masterpiece of wordprocessing that they spent an hour on in the last lesson. Encourage your children to find sensible and informative names for their documents. The best document names give some indication of the content of the writing, and also perhaps a hint of the writer's name. This problem can be further overcome by getting your students to set up

an individual folder on the computer in which to save their work.

Useful wordprocessing functions

The functions described below are all fairly basic ones, and if you are reasonably computer literate you may wish to skip this section. Most of these functions are connected to the layout of a document, and throughout I refer to the most commonly used wordprocessing program, Microsoft Word (apologies to the Apple Mac users out there). I hope that you will find at least one function below that you have not yet thought about using.

- *Positioning functions*: On the toolbar towards the top of the screen there are four main options for positioning your text on the page. These are left align, centre, right align and justify. In addition, the tab button on the upper left of the keyboard is very useful for positioning words on the page. Do encourage your students not to position anything with the spacebar!
- *Changing text appearance*: Just to the left of the positioning functions, there are three buttons that allow you to add bold, italics or underlining to your writing. Alternatively, you can highlight the relevant text and use the shortcuts of Ctrl+B, Ctrl+I, and Ctrl+U. There are also two pull-down menus of different fonts and text sizes to the left of these buttons (in the later versions of Word these fonts are displayed as they appear on the page). It is normally better to type the text first, then highlight the words that you wish to change. On the 'Format' menu under 'Font' you will also find various different options for changing the appearance of your text, including its size, appearance, font and colour.
- *Changing the page appearance*: Adding borders to your page, or to a section of text, can make your students' writing look much more interesting (although do bear in mind the amount of printer ink these will use up). You can find this function on the pull-down menu called 'Format', under 'Borders and shading'. As well as the more straightforward borders, there is also an 'Art' section which offers some

interesting alternatives. These 'Art' borders are excellent for using on worksheets.

- *Columns*: The use of columns seems to be an area of difficulty for many children, but they are extremely useful when writing in a newspaper style. You will find the function on the 'Format' menu. Do advise your students that further columns will appear automatically when they have typed to the end of the first column. When typing a newspaper article, it is a good idea to put a line between each column, to make it easier to read. This line can be added by ticking a box on the 'Columns' menu.

- *Toolbars*: On the 'View' pull-down menu, you can find a number of toolbars that are not normally displayed. These include a 'WordArt' toolbar, on which you can find some useful ready-designed WordArt titles. I would recommend that you display the 'Drawing' toolbar at all times – it includes functions for changing text and background colour, as well as arrows and other autoshapes that can prove very helpful when writing essay plans and creating other diagrams.

- *Adding symbols*: If you look at the 'Insert' pull-down menu, and then click on 'Symbol', you will find a wide range of really useful options. These 'Symbol' menus include fractions, Arabic letters, copyright symbols, and so on.

Tips for effective wordprocessing

I am fortunate in that I worked with computers in an office long before I became a teacher. I was trained to wordprocess documents, and I also learned how to touch-type. In fact I would advise any teacher who has the time, opportunity or inclination to learn how to type properly. It makes creating worksheets a far quicker task, and is also very useful when it comes to writing computerized reports. Here are a few tips that will help you and your students use the wordprocessor more effectively.

- *Write first, format last*: It is incredibly tempting for our students to spend vast quantities of time 'prettying up' their work as they write: changing fonts and text sizes, adding colours and shading, applying borders, and so on. However, it is always best to encourage your students to type the content first, and only then consider the presentation. There are a couple of reasons for this. First, it means that the content of the writing is done without excessive amounts of time being lost on formatting. Second, you might have noticed how 'glitches' sometimes appear on the page, points at which the formatting changes for no apparent reason. For instance, if you select a new font, the computer may drop back into the default font (usually Times New Roman). This can result in very strange changes of font within a document. You can help your students avoid these glitches by using the 'Select All' function on the 'Edit' menu, and then changing the font *after* they have finished the work.

- *Save, save, save*: I'm sure that you too have had that awful experience where a child tells you 'my computer just froze/ crashed and I lost all my work'. This problem can be overcome by encouraging your children to name and save their documents right from the word go. When I am working on computers with a class, I spend the first ten minutes going around to check that everyone has named and saved their work. It is also a good idea to tell your children to save their work every few minutes, as they work.

- *Use the 'Ctrl' functions*: Microsoft Word offers the user a variety of shortcuts for the most commonly used functions, such as save, bold, italic, etc. These shortcuts are, in my experience, largely ignored by students in favour of the pull-down menus at the top of the screen. However, these shortcut keys can save a great deal of time, particularly Ctrl+S for saving a document as you go along. (In fact, this should become an automatic reflex every few minutes when writing on a computer.) These shortcuts are listed on the pull-down menus.

The computer as a writing tool

There is a danger that we miss out on the full potential of the computer as a tool for writing. We might see it as a way for our children to 'type up' written work, or our students write a piece by simply starting at the beginning and stopping when they get to the end. Computers offer us a very powerful tool for structuring, editing and working with our writing, without the need to rewrite by hand. Here are some ideas about how you might use the computer as an active tool, rather than simply as a passive receptor of text.

- *Outlining*: Ask your children to create an outline of their work on the computer, before they start to write. This might mean putting a series of headings, or it could be putting a single word or phrase that describes what will go into each paragraph. When writing a story, they might write a series of sentences that describe each different event or section of the story, before filling in the details.

- *Editing*: One of the most wonderful things about writing on a computer is the ability it offers to move text around with ease. Spend time getting your children familiar with the ways in which they can cut, paste and copy on the computer. These functions are at the top left of the screen, represented by the symbols of scissors (cut), paper (copy) and clipboard (paste). They can also be found on the pull-down 'Edit' menu, or can be used with the shortcuts of Ctrl+X, Ctrl+C and Ctrl+V. Your children may also need to be taught how to block their work. This can be quite a challenge for them, as it requires a reasonably high degree of dexterity with the mouse. A good way of blocking single lines is to click the mouse once, with the cursor positioned just to the side of that line of text.

- *Checking technique*: Another extremely useful function of writing on a computer is the ability to check the accuracy of your work. On the 'Tools' menu you will find the function for checking spelling and grammar, or you can use the F7 button as a shortcut. Shift+F7 is also a useful shortcut for the thesaurus.

Maximizing your ICT resources

The majority of schools now have a reasonable level of ICT resources. However, there will still be situations where a number of teachers are sharing a few computers between their classes, or where a class of thirty students will have to make do with one machine per pair or even much less. Here are some thoughts about how you can maximize your ICT resources, especially if they are limited.

- *Sharing computers*: This can be a recipe for disaster unless it is well managed by the teacher. If you do need your children to share computers, then the following advice will help.
  - Set the boundaries for your children before work starts – this will avoid time wasted on settling disputes.
  - Warn the children that they will need to take it in turns to write, and specify how this will happen.
  - One approach is to allow each child ten minutes at a time, before swapping over.
  - You might divide the lesson time in half instead, for instance giving each child thirty minutes of a lesson that is one hour long.
  - Be aware that the child who is not 'hands on' at the computer must still have a sense of involvement in the task.
  - Alternatively, set a separate non-computer task for those children who are not on a machine.
- *Reader and writer*: If your children are using the computer to type up work that has already been written down by hand, one of them can act as reader while the other types the words. Doing this helps develop other skills: the reader is practising reading out loud, while the writer will have to consider how the words that she hears are spelt.
- *Typing together*: If you feel that paired sharing of computers is not suitable for your children, you could ask them to type together. Depending on how slow they are, this might mean each child typing a word in turn, or perhaps a line or paragraph.
- *The computer as reward*: For many children using ICT is a highly motivational activity, especially for those who do not have access to a computer at home. Make use of the fact that time on the computer is viewed so positively and, if you have limited access to machines, make this a 'reward' for those who behave or work well. Obviously, you will need to

ensure curriculum entitlement for all. However, you will generally find that all your children want to earn this 'reward' and are willing to work hard to receive it.

- *Make it count*: If your access to ICT facilities is limited, make sure that the time you do spend on computers really counts. Consider how important the presentational aspects are, and whether it might be more worthwhile to use the time to practise editing and 'building' the writing.

- *Book well ahead*: There is nothing more frustrating than wanting to use a computer room but finding it booked up for months ahead. Your school or ICT department probably runs a booking system for any computer rooms, and my advice would be to get in early with your booking. Halfway into a term, when the teachers are feeling like a few well-deserved lessons off, the computer room can seem remarkably appealing and any free space will be quickly snapped up!

- *Take care of the machines you do have*: With limited ICT resources, every computer counts. Spend time explaining to your children how to take care of the machines – what to do if they crash, which parts are particularly fragile and should be handled with care, and so on. For instance, the CD ROM drive often takes a battering from negligent or poorly behaved children. Insist that they treat the school machines as they would a computer in their own home.

The internet in the classroom

We are really in the infancy of the use of the internet in education, and many of us are still unsure about what it offers us in terms of true educational value. There are so many different websites springing up (and going out of business) that it is very time-consuming to search for those that are worth a visit. When companies first started developing educational sites for the net, some of these were subscription-based, and schools had to pay to access them. Although there are still some of these subscription sites around, there are also many free sites now available to the teacher. Here are some thoughts about using the internet in the classroom.

- *There's no such thing as a free lunch*: Even the 'free' sites need to be funded in some way, in order to afford to run, and to produce good-quality content. There are sites out there that are not funded by advertising, but do be aware that someone, somewhere is paying for the site to exist.

- *Be aware of advertising*: As teachers we need to be aware of the adverts to which we expose our children, both their number and their content. When planning work that involves using the internet, it is a good idea to check the sites first to find out how obtrusive the advertising is.

- *Find a good search engine*: A good-quality search engine will save you time and effort. It will also help you find relevant content for use in specific curriculum areas. I use Google, as I find that it brings up good, clear results and is straightforward to use.

- *Learn more about the 'net'*: There are some excellent books available that can help make your use of the internet more effective, and which give you information about the more technical aspects of the worldwide web. I would recommend two books in particular to teachers who are using the internet in their classrooms. These are *The Internet in Schools* by Duncan Grey (Continuum, 2000), and *The Rough Guide to the Internet* by Peter Buckley and Duncan Clark (Rough Guides, 2003).

- *Utilize your school website*: Many schools now have websites of their own. If this is the case with your school, see if it is possible for you and your children to provide content for the site.

- *Set up your own website*: If your school does not have a site of its own, or if you are feeling brave, why not have a go at setting up your own website? I recently decided that I needed to set up my own author website. Before I started, I had absolutely no idea what I was doing, but I found the whole process surprisingly straightforward. There is no real need for you to be able to write (or even understand) HTML in order to create your own site. There are software programs out there that will basically do it all for you, and the moment of 'publishing' your site to the net gives a wonderful feeling of achievement. All you really need in order to write your own website is the ability to wordprocess a document, and perhaps a friendly colleague who has a bit of experience with ICT.

Email

The email is a very recent addition to the world of written communication. Not quite a letter, not quite a text message, the email is rapidly becoming a written form all of its own. There is quite a high level of informality in the email at present – we tend to use different vocabulary to that which we might use in a letter. The use of abbreviations (such as 'LOL') and 'emoticons' (such as ☺) is all part of this informality. In addition, correspondence between friends often does away with the need for 'proper' technique – punctuation, capital letters, paragraphing, and so on.

There is much potential in the email for teachers interested in developing literacy. Here are just a couple of ideas to get you started.

- *School/home communication*: Many children now have access to email via a home computer. If this is the case with your students, you could email them with homework reminders, or with comments on their work and behaviour.
- *Chain stories*: You might use emails between your students in which they write a 'chain story', each adding a sentence in turn, as they receive the message.

Safety on the internet

One of the things that makes the internet such a wonderful resource is the fact that it can be used by anyone and everyone, as long as they have access to a computer with a modem. However, this also has its disadvantages. Our children can communicate with other people very easily, and it is all too easy for these people to pretend to be someone else. We have all heard the horror stories of children being abused via contacts made on the internet. Although there are filtering programs available, it is better to be safe than sorry, especially at this stage in the development of the technology. Here are some tips about 'net safety' for you to share with your class.

- *Keep personal information personal*: Warn your children about the dangers of giving out personal information on the net, particularly if they are using chatrooms. Tell them they should never give out their age, telephone number or address under any circumstances. If they do wish to use their real name, they should stick to using their first name only.
- *Virtual people*: On the internet, we are 'virtual', we exist in cyberspace in the form that we choose to reveal. Warn your students that the people they communicate with via the internet could be using a false persona. For instance it is perfectly simple for a fifty-year-old man to claim that he is a fifteen-year-old boy, with all the potential abuses that might result.
- *Never arrange meetings*: Because of this potential for dishonesty, make it clear to your students that they should never arrange meetings in person with the other users they meet on the internet.
- *Viruses*: Although we know about computer viruses swishing around the net, there is still a real temptation to download material that could be infected. This might mean opening an attachment that comes with an email, it could be downloading a picture or program from the net. Explain to your children the potential damage that can be done when downloading from the internet.
- *Access to adult sites*: Be fully aware that when your children use the internet, it is likely that some of them will try to access adult, or porn, sites. Even the best filtering software cannot always prevent this from happening. And children being children will of course be interested to see what exciting 'adult' material they might be able to access. Keep a close eye out for any of your students doing this and, if you suspect an individual, check the history log of their internet use after they have finished with the machine.

13 Celebrating writing

Some children simply don't view writing as an exciting facet of their lives. For the weak or the demotivated, it can be a grind, a daily challenge that they must submit themselves to throughout their schooling. This final chapter is about challenging that assumption: about finding ways to celebrate writing, and making it a joyful and exciting prospect. Although some of the suggestions below may take up quite a lot of your time in preparation and organization, the results in terms of motivation, behaviour and inspiration will almost always be worth the effort. Many of the ideas below are ones that I have used or been part of during my teaching career. They stick in my mind as very positive times in my school life, and I am certain that the same applies for the children who were involved.

Publishing writing

Having their work published can be an incredibly motivating experience for young writers. For every piece that we write there will be an audience, or even a number of audiences. At the simplest level, the audience for the majority of classroom writing will be the teacher. Some pieces of writing will have a wider audience, for instance those that are put on display, or that are sent home to parents. The widest audience of all can be found for those pieces of work that are 'published' in some way. There are a wide range of forms in which you might publish your children's work. Here are just a few ideas.

- *On the internet*: Writing that is published on the internet has a huge potential audience. Having a piece of their work published on the web will help to motivate your students, and is an excellent way of celebrating writing.

- *On your classroom walls*: Although we might not really view it as 'publishing' our children's work, displaying their writing on the classroom walls is in fact a form of public celebration.
- *Via a competition*: Setting up a whole-school writing competition, as described below and in Chapter 1 (p.9), offers a great way of publishing writing. The audience for this will include the school students and staff, and also the parents.
- *Via a school magazine*: If you are a keen writer and editor yourself, you might consider setting up a school magazine. School magazines seem to be less prevalent these days than in the past (perhaps because teachers are snowed under with other work). However, I can remember to this day the excitement that was generated by seeing my own work published in this way as a child.
- *Creating 'books'*: A project in which your students create their own books, from first idea to final product, would be an excellent way of celebrating their writing (not only story books, but also books in all areas of the curriculum). These books might be aimed at an audience of younger students within your school, or perhaps even for a more general audience via the school library.

Book weeks

A 'book week' is an excellent way to get the whole school celebrating reading, writing and books in general. An organization called Booktrust organizes an annual book week in the UK, which takes place in the first full week of October. (You can find details of the Booktrust websites in Appendix 2 at the back of this book.) Although a book week might be organized by an English coordinator in the primary school, or by the English Department in a secondary school, there is no reason why it should not take place on a cross-curricular basis.

During book week, the focus could be on both reading and writing, perhaps with children writing their own books in the style of their favourite authors. You might get local companies to sponsor your school in buying books, or ask local librarians to come in with a selection of books from the libraries in your area.

Author days/weeks

A day or week dedicated to one author is a great opportunity to get your students reading and writing in earnest. For instance, in my first school the English Department organized a Shakespeare Day. Many of the teachers dressed up as characters from the plays, and performed scenes to the students. The children were involved in different writing activities, including creating Shakespearean love poems. By raising the profile of an author in this way, you also raise the profile of writers and books in general. There is no need, of course, to stick to writers from the past. For instance, I am certain that a 'Harry Potter' day or week would go down extremely well in both primary and secondary schools.

Charity activities

Children love the chance to 'make a difference', to raise money for a cause that is close to their hearts. Many schools already take part in Red Nose Day or the Children in Need appeal. When developing charity activities for these times, consider the role that writing might play. For instance, there could be a sponsored write as well as the more typical sponsored read. The children might be allowed to 'set lines' for their teachers, and sponsor them for writing out their lines a hundred or a thousand times.

Competitions

Why not capitalize on the competitive streak that seems to run through many of our youngsters? In Chapter 1 (p.9), I describe a poetry competition that I set up in school. I was inundated with entries, and I published the winning and highly commended entries in a booklet. This was then sold to children and parents to help fund the prizes of book tokens. Your competition might be in a subject other than English, for instance a science competition for the best design and instructions for building a space rocket.

Writers' workshops

There are many professional writers who are able to provide

workshops for schools. These might be about storytelling, poetry, writing from other cultures, and so on. In my experience, having an 'expert' come in from outside the school is very good in motivating the students with their work. You can find details of writers who provide school workshops via the internet.

'Play in a day'

It can be a wonderful experience to write alongside your students, and one way of doing this is to organize a 'Play in a day'. This could take place at the end of term, when the whole school is off timetable, for instance on an activity day. The basic format is that the teacher and students work together to produce a play in only one day, using a specified theme or the outline of a story. They then present this play to the rest of the school, perhaps on the last day of term. The great thing about this exercise is that most of the 'writing' will take place through improvisation, and it is therefore very suitable for children who struggle with putting their thoughts down on paper.

Trips

Trips can be a great way of inspiring good writing. The children will be visiting new places, seeing new things, and will actually *want* to make a written record of their trip after the event. For instance, you might take your class to a local festival, and this could inspire some descriptive writing about what they have seen. You could take them to a museum and ask them to write about one of the exhibits. For many children, a trip is one of the most memorable and exciting events in their school career.

Part 5

Resources for Writing

Appendix 1 Text-messaging

As I have emphasized throughout this book, if we want to motivate our students to write, the work that we set must be topical and fun. And what could be more topical than text-messaging? Here is a list of some of the more common text-message abbreviations. Many of these terms are simply the shortest possible phonic abbreviations, often using numbers such as 4 and 8 for their sounds. Alternatively, some use acronyms to replace commonly used phrases. These abbreviations are also becoming commonly used in emails and in postings on the internet.

All the best	ATB
Are you OK	RUOK?
Are	R
Be	B
Before	B4
Be seeing you	BCNU
Bye bye for now	BB4N
Cutie	QT
Date	D8
Easy	EZ
Excellent	XLNT
For	4
For your information	FYI
Great	GR8
If you know what I mean	IFKWIM
In my opinion	IMO
Later	L8R
Laugh out loud	LOL
Oh I see	OIC

Please call me	PCM
See you later	CU L8R
Thanks	THX
To/too	2
Today	2DAY
Tomorrow	2MORO
Tonight	2NITE
Want to	WAN2
Why	Y
You	U

For further information about text-messaging, and more abbreviations, you could try:

WAN2TLK? Ltle Bk of Txt Msgs and the accompanying series. (London: Michael O'Mara, 2003)

Or look at the following web pages:
www.bbc.co.uk/joyoftext/

www.askoxford.com/betterwriting/emoticons
This page gives a list of emoticons (email/text symbols that indicate emotion) as well as a dictionary of text-message abbreviations.

Appendix 2 Useful websites

The list of websites given below covers a range of sites dealing with the written word. I have tried, as far as possible, to include only websites that have been running for a substantial amount of time, or which are backed up by large organizations, and are therefore likely to remain online. I have also tried to 'weed out' the sites that subject you to those irritating pop-up adverts, or which are overly commercial.

General

www.standards.dfes.gov.uk/literacy/
Up-to-date information on literacy and the National Literacy Strategy.

www.standards.dfes.gov.uk/literacy/teaching_resources/nls_framework/
The framework of the National Literacy Strategy, which includes a useful glossary of literacy terms.

www.nate.org.uk
The website of the National Association for the Teaching of English.

Writing resources

www.askoxford.com
The website of the Oxford University Press. Sections on 'The World of Words' and 'Better Writing'.

www.edufind.com/english/grammar
A very useful directory of grammatical terminology.

www.word-detective.com
The Word Detective site, which offers entertaining discussions about the origin and meaning of words.

www.blewa.co.uk
A project on writing and the written word, run by the British Library.

www.wordpool.co.uk
A useful website which includes lots of articles about writing for children, a list of children's books, and also author profiles and contact details.

Teaching resources

www.teachit.co.uk
A free library of English resources, useful for secondary teachers.

www.teachingideas.co.uk
An excellent resource with lots of ideas for teaching English at primary school level.

www.teachingtips.co.uk
A site for secondary teachers, run by Longman Pearson.

Story writing

www.the-phone-book.com
A showcase for short and ultra-short stories written for WAP mobile phones.

Publishing your children's writing

www.teachit.co.uk
A place to publish your children's work, plus lots of really useful teaching resources.

www.kotn.ntu.ac.uk
'Kids on the net' is a website run by Nottingham Trent University, which publishes a range of children's writing online.

www.thescriptorium.net
A great site run by Sherry Ramsey, a Canadian writer. There is a special section for young writers called 'Scriptorium Scribbles'.

Children's books and authors

www.booktrust.org.uk
The site of the Book Trust, which runs the National Children's book week.

www.booktrusted.com
A second Book Trust site, dedicated to children's literature.

www.ncll.org.uk
The site of the National Centre for Language and Literacy. This site has an author database where you can search for an author willing to visit your school.

Writing to penpals

When using the internet to communicate with schools and students around the world, teachers do need to be aware of the safety issues involved. I would strongly recommend that you talk to your children about sensible behaviour on the internet. You can find more information about this in Chapter 12.

www.epals.com
An excellent site, with clear design and a strong international focus. Strongly safety conscious.

www.teaching.com/keypals
A clear site, with unobtrusive advertising.

www.agirlsworld.com/penpal/index.html
A colourful, fun site, but only for girls and with quite an American slant.

Special educational needs

www.dyslexia-inst.org.uk
The website of The Dyslexia Institute.

www.bda-dyslexia.org.uk
The website of The British Dyslexia Association.

Appendix 3 Vocabulary

The lists in this appendix provide some useful vocabulary for written work. For subject-specific words, see Chapter 7, which deals with writing across the curriculum. You might like to use these lists to introduce key terms, or to set spelling tests for your students. I have included a list of some of the most commonly used words, which will be useful for teaching and consolidating vocabulary at both primary and secondary level. I have also included a list of words that, in my experience, cause particular problems for older students.

Commonly used words

a, about, across, after, again, all, almost, among, an, and, any, as, at, be, because, before, between, by, come, do, down, enough, even, ever, every, far, for, forward, from, get, give, go, have, he, hear, here, how, I, if, in, keep, let, little, make, may, me, much, near, no, not, now, of, off, on, only, or, other, our, out, over, please, put, quite, said, say, see, seem, send, she, so, some, still, such, take, than, that, the, then, there, this, though, through, to, together, tomorrow, under, up, very, well, when, where, while, who, why, will, with, yes, yesterday, you, your

Commonly used nouns

ant, apple, arm, baby, bag, ball, band, basket, bath, bed, bee, bell, bird, board, boat, book, boot, bottle, box, boy, branch, brick, bridge, brush, bucket, button, cake, camera, card, cart, cat, chain, cheese, chin, church, circle, clock, cloud, coat, collar, cow, cup, curtain, cushion, dog, door, drawer, dress, ear, egg, engine, eye, face, farm, feather, finger, fish, flag, floor, fly, foot, fork, garden, girl, glove, hair, hand, hat, head, heart, horse, hospital, house, island, jewel, kettle, key, knee, knife, leaf, leg, library, line, lip, lock, map, match, monkey, moon, mouth, nail, neck, needle, net, nose, nut, office, orange, oven, parcel, pen, pencil, picture, pig, pin, plane, plate, pocket, pot, potato, rail, rat, ring, roof, root, sail, school, scissors, sheep, shelf, ship, shirt, shoe, skirt, snake, sock, spade, spoon, square, stamp, star, station, stick, stomach, street, sun, table, tail, thumb, ticket, toe, tooth, town, train, tree, trousers, umbrella, wall, watch, wheel, window, wing, worm

Problem words for older students

accommodation, beautiful, beginning, cautious, competition, definitely, desperate, disguise, exaggerate, explanation, extraordinary, February, frightened, laughter, occasion, opinion, particularly, patiently, prejudice, privilege, separate, successfully, suspicious

English

Linguistic analysis
alliteration, atmosphere, cliché, comparison, expression, figurative, imagery, metaphor, onomatopoeia, personification, simile

Spelling, punctuation and grammar
apostrophe, clause, comma, conjunction, consonant, exclamation, homonym, paragraph, plural, prefix, preposition, subordinate, suffix, synonym, vocabulary, vowel

Writing about texts
advertise, advertisement, chorus, climax, dialogue, genre, myth, narrative, narrator, opinion, pamphlet, playwright, rehearse, resolution, rhyme, scene, significant, soliloquy, tabloid

Writing about characters
ambitious, cautious, character, characterization, courageous, despised, disguise, enemies, foolish, hypocritical, notorious, obedient, rebellious, relationship, serious, vicious

Letter writing
apologize, complain, enquire, faithfully, forward, information, madam, receive, sincerely, writing

Appendix 4 Marking symbols

The marking symbols given below can be used by the teacher for marking written work, and also by the students when editing their writing.

~~	Expression/grammar is incorrect
____	Spelling mistake/word is wrong
//	Insert paragraph
∧	Word missing/insert word or letter
O	Punctuation missing
?	Unclear/don't understand what is meant
/	Cut letter/punctuation
✓	Good section
✓✓	Excellent section

Index

writing, *continued*
   see also creative writing;
      computers, writing on;
      developing writing skills;
      fiction writing; non-fiction
      writing; poetry writing; script
      writing; subject areas and
      writing

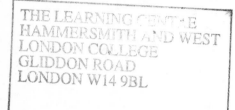

THE LEARNING CENTRE
HAMMERSMITH AND WEST
LONDON COLLEGE
GLIDDON ROAD
LONDON W14 9BL